A MONKEY'S ORIENTATION

A MONKEY'S ORIENTATION

Cris Rogers

Authentic

MILTON KEYNES ● COLORADO SPRINGS ● HYDERABAD

First published in 2008 by Authentic Media
9 Holdom Avenue, Bletchley, Milton Keynes, Bucks, MK1 1QR, UK
1820 Jet Stream Drive, Colorado Springs, CO 80921, USA
OM Authentic Media, Medchal Road, Jeedimetla Village,
Secunderabad 500 055, A.P., India
www.authenticmedia.co.uk
Authentic Media is a division of IBS-STL U.K., limited by
guarantee, with its Registered Office at Kingstown Broadway,
Carlisle, Cumbria CA3 0HA. Registered in England & Wales No.
1216232. Registered charity 270162

British Library Cataloguing in Publication Data
A catalogue record for this book is available from the
British Library

ISBN-13: 978-1-85078-782-2

Cover Design by Moose77
Printed and bound in Great Britain

THANK YOU

Beki – thank you for encouraging me to write, without your support and love this would have never even made it from my notebook.

Isaac and Daisy – you remind me each day how sacred life is and how holy breakfast and milkshakes can really be. You are both wonderful and amazing children: please never change.

Dad – you have been a fantastic role model, and I am who I am because of you: thank you for always being there.

Soul Survivor Church, Harrow – thank you for allowing me to journey with you in becoming a community that leaves religion behind and follows Jesus.

Mark, Lyd, Ben, Emma and Mac – you have been an amazing support and shown real love and care, thank you.

And finally Grandad – see you soon!

OUTLINE

FOREWORD

Cris has written a great book here. *A Monkey's Orientation* is funny, insightful, biblical, helpful and inspiring. You will find within these pages liberating truths communicated in an accessible way. Many of us have badly misunderstood the meaning of the biblical call to holy living. That which was meant to liberate us has instead enslaved us. I talk to many young people who think that Christian living is a rule book, a list of do's and don'ts. As a result they constantly feel guilty because of their failure to pass the holiness exam. No wonder many give up. Real Christianity does not start with a big 'do' but with a big 'done'. 'It is finished,' declared Jesus from the cross and our life with him is all about entering into his rest. We begin by sitting in the heavenly places 'in Christ' before we can hope to 'walk in the Spirit' or 'stand against the devil'.

This book unpacks the great truth that what we do flows from who we are. In other words we were created to be human beings not human doings! Cris does this with some great theological nuggets and explains the context of certain Bible stories brilliantly. This is great teaching but also very practical. It will not just inform your mind or warm your heart but, more importantly, affect the way you live.

It is my prayer that as you read these pages you will realise afresh what amazingly good news the good news of Jesus is. Revelation leads to transformation. The revelation contained in this book has the power to change your life.

Enjoy!

Mike Pilavachi
November 2007

INTRO: RADAR |00

Do you know how tricky it is to come up with a decent title for a book? This one almost defeated me. It's not like I lost sleep over it – it was my newborn daughter that did that – but no title seemed to fit.

I didn't want to simply call it *Holiness or Living a Life of Holiness*: they were far too obvious. I wanted something cheeky and intriguing, perhaps mysterious. We even came up with *Are You Doing the Monkey Dance?* but thought this would completely stop anyone buying it.

So we made our decision – and then I told my brother it was going to be called *A Monkey's Orientation*. He thought it was going to be a book about homosexual monkeys. Please be reassured that this isn't about how monkeys should and shouldn't behave with other male or female monkeys: I am no monkey specialist and will never set myself up as one. I am sure there are other books you can buy on this topic and I apologise if you bought this book thinking that.

Another friend misheard and thought it was called *Monkey Orienteering* and wondered why I had written a book about monkeys running through the countryside with maps.

You might still be wondering why it has such a strange title – for an answer you will have to wait until a later chapter. So what is it about? *A Monkey's Orientation* is an exploration of how holiness comes as a response to God: who we turn our lives towards. We will do this by digging deep into Jesus' faith and understanding the scriptures he read. As we start this journey, it's important to stress something often overlooked. Jesus was Jewish.

In my job as a youth pastor I often find myself explaining that Jesus and his followers were committed Jews (for more information, see the appendix at the back of the book). Jesus' teaching reflects his Jewish heritage: to comprehend much of the New Testament we need to take a brief look at Jewish texts and the culture of two thousand years ago in the Middle East. No iPods, no McDonald's, no football and certainly no *Lost*, *The O.C.* or *Neighbours*.

We will explore Jesus' understanding of holiness from his Jewish tradition – spending much of our time trying to breathe some life into those old stories found in the first half of the Bible, hoping and praying they breathe new life into us.

One more thing before we dive in: I was recently sat having a coffee with a female friend of mine, who believes she is very intuitive when it comes to men. Suddenly she pointed at a guy walking by and said 'He's free!' What do you say to such a comment? I politely nodded and tried to return to our previous conversation. 'He's free!' There she went again, pointing at random strangers, claiming that she knew their relationship status. Emma explained how being single and intuitive gave her this gift called 'guy-dar' which allowed her to spot any single guy around.

Only a short time later I was talking with a friend when he suddenly said, 'It's a new reg.' It seemed that this friend has the gift of spotting cars with new registration plates – I have no idea what use that is. Another friend told me that he knows someone who has pay-dar and that she was able to accurately guess someone's pay band.

This got me thinking about what was on my radar. If I am honest I think it must be celebrities (celeb-dar). Every time I go to London I always seem to spot someone. Ant and Dec in a department store, Ricky Gervais in a supermarket, Stephen Merchant outside the Hard Rock Café and lots of odd people from *The X Factor*.

The early Christians' approach to God is like their 'God-dar'. They had the ability to see and recognise God in the things around them and in all that they did.

Many of us have these radars that scan the world around us, so why is it that we often only turn on our God-dar in church on a Sunday? It is as though it turns on automatically when the service starts and then off again the moment the service ends. Is it because we don't realise that God is in the world and that everything is sacred because of this?[1]

There is a fantastic story of a young guy called Samuel who was training to be leader in the Temple. One night, he is fast asleep when suddenly he is woken up by God's voice. Samuel has no idea who is speaking to him so presumes that it is his boss in the next room. He goes through to Eli who is sleeping and hasn't called Samuel. This happens three times, before Eli suggests to Samuel that it may be God calling him.

Samuel has his radar on slightly, but still has no idea who is trying to talk to him. (If you want to read more the story is in 1 Samuel 3.) How often does God try to speak to you but when you hear him you think it is someone or something else?

I am not claiming that if you have God-dar on you will be hearing voices in your sleep, but I am sure that God is speaking and acting constantly and we are totally unaware that he is even there. When Samuel eventually realises that it is God speaking to him he hears an amazing message that changes his life forever.

As we start this journey together why not turn on your God-dar and see if he is saying anything to you. Many people believe that at certain times God tries to reveal something new and fresh to us.

Let's turn our God-dar on and see where we end up.

Please bear in mind when reading . . .

In the Old Testament, God declared his name to be 'I am who I am.' Because this name is so holy and so sacred it is translated in our Bibles as 'LORD', never uncapitalised. Where this name is in Bible quotes I have used YHVH to indicate the holy name of God, and not just a man of high ranking, which is 'Lord'.

REDEFINING
HOLINESS | 01

HOLINESS IS A FUNNY THING

Nuns	– Holy
Cliff Richard	– Holy
War	– Unholy
Fair Trade	– Holy
Slavery	– Unholy
Cheese & Onion crisps	– Semi-holy
Golf	– n/a
PCs	– Unholy
Macs	– Holy
Marmite	– Very unholy

Holiness is a funny thing. If I asked you to decide which of the above list were holy or unholy, you might have opposing answers to me. We will each decide differently depending on our ideas about what holiness means. So why is it that we might have to have a discussion about whether Cliff Richard, Mac computers and Marmite are holy or not, but I bet we all agree that nuns are holy? We all have our own sometimes vague ideas about what this eight-letter word does and doesn't mean, but at the same time we use it to describe an attribute of God and something we need to aspire to. All too often it's seen as something those goody-two-shoes Christians are.

But is it really true that holiness is something that only nuns and Sunday school teachers with blue rinses are able to acquire? This is exactly what I thought for years, which certainly didn't help me with my own lifestyle issues, being neither a nun nor over sixty with blue hair.

THAT AWFUL SERMON

At the age of fifteen I found myself watching *The Sound of Music* with my girlfriend's family. This film did nothing but seriously disfigure my view of what the monastic lifestyle was all about. In my mind, the film somehow connected the monastic lifestyle with entering singing competitions, falling in love with wealthy men and legging it over the Austrian hills scared to death because the hills were alive with the sound of music.

Just a few weeks before I watched the film, one of the leaders at my church spoke to us on the topic of 'Nuns' holiness and how we must try to emulate it'. As I sat there on the sofa watching Maria, the words 'Not for me' were going through my head. I totally understand the intention of the speaker but when your only example of the monastic lifestyle is not a particularly holy one, it all seems a bit unhelpful.

There were other things said in this rather long sermon that left me confused. The speaker said that we needed to claim holiness and take it for ourselves. This made me think that holiness could be bought in a cosmic religious superstore perhaps alongside meekness and the gift of tongues. The only way I could imagine to 'claim' it would be to pick it up in the supermarket, put it in the trolley and pay for it at the checkout, just like you'd do with a can of tinned vegetables from the third shelf down on aisle 14 at Asda. Was this what they meant when they said we had to take it for ourselves? I wasn't sure that it was, because our local supermarket didn't sell anything even vaguely like tinned holiness and when I looked over to my dad for some kind of clue, he looked back just as puzzled as I was.

Rushing home after what was a very confusing evening service, I decided to look up this word 'holiness' to see what it was all about. After flicking through Chambers dictionary for a few minutes, I found the word I was looking for. Somewhat unhelpfully it read 'The noun holiness has one meaning: to possess the quality of being holy.' Hardly blinding me with science! Still not any clearer on what holiness actually meant, I carried this idea of Maria the Nun somehow being linked to holiness right through my school and university years.

Not long after I finished university, I was forced to rethink holiness again. I found myself being invited to speak at a church near one of my favourite surf beaches at a British youth event called 'Naked'. The topic I had been given to speak on was 'What does it mean to be a Christian?' Sweeping titles like that tend to confuse me and although I said I'd do the talk, I spent the months leading up to the event watching DVDs to keep my mind off the preparation I should have been doing. I even alphabetised my CD collection. Which is how I ended up sitting in front of my computer with just seven days to go until the event, still with no clue of what I was going to say. So, out of sheer desperation I typed eight words into Google: 'What does it mean to be a Christian?'

For those of you who have been hidden away from the computer age reading Enid Blyton books and sleeping – Google is a search engine that looks at eight billion websites to help you find sites that contain the words you are looking for. 'What does it mean to be a Christian?' apparently appeared on 51.2 million websites. The screen in front of me had a list of the first seven sites containing those words. I browsed through the list until I saw the fifth website. Doing a double take, I leaned in closer to check I'd read it right. After re-reading I was pretty sure Google must have made a mistake. Checking my search, I re-typed 'What does it mean to be a Christian?' Again the site appeared, practically begging me to check it out.

Now, I don't wish to talk about this website to shock anyone or to cause them to stumble in their faith, especially in a book on holiness but I think it's important that I get this off my chest.

Checking over my shoulder to make sure there was no one watching me, I moved my mouse over to the link and clicked on it.

Fig Leaf Forum provides fellowship, edification and encouragement to Bible-believing Christian nudists and naturists through its online ministry.[2]

Surely nudism and naturism can't ever go alongside Christianity?

This definitely wasn't something I'd been taught in Sunday school by my holy blue-haired eighty-four-year-old teacher Mrs Metcalf. Yet, as I spent a little time reading through the Fig Leaf Forum website I started to think that maybe there was something in this Christian nudism that I quite liked. Just to clarify, being a naturist doesn't appeal to me at all but it was something about the idea of being free from the clothing and masks of this world that started me on my journey towards redefining holiness for myself.

STRIPPING BACK

The Christians on this website claimed that being nude made them feel closer to God as this was the way God intended people to be in the beginning. Others talked about being set free from having to look good and dress well, presenting something they weren't to the world. In a strange way I could see very clearly what they were talking about. There are some days when I fancy not shaving, wearing my Busted T-shirt and having my hair 'get up and go' chic. The stress of having to present myself to the world is just too much on some Monday mornings and if I could go to the office wearing nothing but my lobster pyjamas, it would probably make me much happier. I guess the guys at my church probably wouldn't appreciate my social comment but I'd be less stressed and more relaxed. Have you ever found yourself wearing clothing a little tight and then spending the day sucking your gut in just to make yourself look better? I know I have and I'm sure I'm not the only one. We spend some days feeling really uncomfortable because we're so worried about what people will think of how we look.

The guys on Fig Leaf Forum had noticed this pressure too. Life had become too much and so, they decided to put a stop to it and just let it all hang out. However, I had no intention of joining Steve from Sheffield or Barbara from Devon on their yearly pilgrimage to a hidden-away nudist colony. No matter how nice the food was or how lovely it was that the local farmer joined them with his home brewed wine, it just wasn't for me. Not to mention the fact that the idea of the sporting activities made me feel a little ill. But the concept of living a life free from the pull of the world was highly compelling. Was it possible to live a nude life without ever needing to take off my clothes? This was something I was willing to investigate.

WHAT WAS HE THINKING?

I started to wonder what God had in mind when he created us. Was it to live the lives we are living? Have we arrived at what God intended or is there more than this? The Christianity I'd been living out for years never fully answered all my lifestyle questions and my faith was about appearing as a 'good' Christian. Like a new toy

missing a part, my life never quite felt like it was working the way it should be. Was this my fault or was I missing the point of what God wanted for me?

I sometimes question what was going through God's
creative mind when he thought up creating Adam and
Eve. Maybe he'd eaten too much cheese the night before
and decided to recreate the weird creatures that had
chased him through his dream? But if, as the Bible says
in Genesis 1:27, we are created in God's image there
must be more to holiness than priests and monks.

It is us who are missing the point of this relationship
with God. Recently God has revealed something new
and fresh to me, something that I wish I had understood
many years before when hearing that sermon on holiness. Holiness is not necessarily about living a monastic
life or about trying to follow a bunch of rules found in
the Old Testament but is more about position and orientation.

THE FAMILY BLESSING

In order to explore this idea of position and orientation,
we can look at the story of Isaac in Genesis 25. When he
reached forty years old, Isaac thought it was about time
he found himself a wife so he married a woman called
Rebekah and they set up home. Unfortunately, Rebekah
was unable to give birth so Isaac prayed that God would
give them a baby. God lavished his blessing upon Isaac
and Rebekah and she became pregnant with twins. The
tradition at this time was that the first-born child would
receive the family blessing, in the same way that today
the eldest child in a royal family will be king one day.
Right from the word go, Rebekah's babies fought – even
while still inside her, which was pretty painful. It was as

if the two babies knew the score and were battling it out to receive the blessing. When the time came for Rebekah to give birth, the Bible says that the one boy was grabbing hold of the other as they came out.

The first child to be born was the 'hunter-gatherer' of the two boys: the strong, manly type. The Bible records that when the child came out he was red – I'm sure his parents freaked out at the sight of a red baby, and with his whole body being covered in hair he was called Esau which literally translates as 'the red hairy one'. Imagine the teacher reading out the register in Hebrew class . . .

David? Here, miss
Mark? Here, miss
Rachel? Here, miss
Red hairy one? YES!

I am so glad by parents called me Cris and not 'tall and bald'.[3]

The second brother, however, was more 'geek chic' and metrosexual[4] than rugby player. This child had the brains but certainly not the brawn and came out right behind his brother with his hand grasping Esau's heel: so he was named Jacob. The name Jacob literally means 'he grasped the heel.' Esau grew to become a strong hairy hunter while Jacob grew up to be the weaker dweeby little brother.

Years passed and when Isaac was old and had lost his sight, he called for his favourite son, the first born, Esau (Gen. 27). Isaac told him to get his harpoon and bow and hunt for some wild boar for him. He then ordered him to cook it and bring it to him to eat, so that he could give Esau his blessing before he died.

Finding out about this conversation and wanting to take the blessing from his brother, Jacob dressed himself as Esau. Wearing his brother's best clothes and placing goats' fur on his body, Jacob took his father's favourite meal to him. Going into his father's presence, Jacob pretended to be his brother to claim the family blessing.

'I am Esau your firstborn. I have done as you told me. Please sit up and eat some of my game so that you may give me your blessing.' Isaac asked his son 'How did you find it so quickly, my son?' Jacob replied 'YHVH your God gave me success'. Isaac evidently had his suspicions, so he asked Jacob to move near so he could touch him and check. Jacob went up to his father who touched him and felt his fake hairy hands and said 'The voice is the voice of Jacob, but the hands are the hands of Esau.' He still wasn't sure, so he checked one last time, asking directly whether Jacob was Esau. Jacob lied and told his father he was.

Then his father said to him, 'Come here, my son, and kiss me.' So Jacob went to him and kissed him. When Isaac caught the smell of his clothes, he blessed him and said

> Ah, the smell of my son
> Is like the smell of a field
> That YHVH has blessed.
> May God give you of heaven's dew
> And of earth's richness
> An abundance of grain and new wine (Gen. 27:27–28).

CLOTHING AND BLESSING

By clothing himself as the son whom the father loved, Jacob was able to get his father's blessing. The son not worthy of the blessing was able to gain it by taking the place of the favourite son. Some of us probably think it's horrible that someone would do this, that Jacob would steal his family blessing away from his brother, to whom it belonged. But this Old Testament story foreshadows what Christ does for us every day with our heavenly Father.

The amazing thing about the story of Jacob and Isaac isn't that it happened once but that it happens today.[5] We need to grasp the truth that holiness and blessing are not related to our performance as a Christian but about where we place ourselves in relation to our Father. Let's look at some Scripture that backs this up.

'You are all sons [and daughters] of God through faith in Christ Jesus, for all of you who were baptised into Christ have clothed yourselves with Christ' (Gal. 3:26–27).

Because of Christ's death on the cross, we are now children of the Creator. Through a personal faith and the freedom from sin that baptism brings, we are now 'clothed' in Christ. Just as Jacob 'clothed' himself with Esau's identity to receive the blessing, we are clothed in Christ's identity and receive God's blessings. This means that our Father looks at us and sees the purity and sinlessness of Jesus rather than our sin and imperfections.

WE BLESS BECAUSE WE HAVE BEEN BLESSED

Growing up as a Christian in a family church, I somehow developed a skewed view of Christianity. I thought that blessing came when you did good things, when you helped people, when you showed love to people. But I've learnt that it's almost the other way round. It's because we've experienced the blessing of the Father, through Jesus, that we should now be blessing others. It's like we're overflowing with the Father's blessing which falls on those around us.

Romans 13:14 talks about the same thing: 'clothe yourselves with the Lord Jesus Christ, and do not think about how to gratify the desires of the sinful nature.'

This passage talks about how to live in the blessing you've received from God – the blessing can only begin when we lay down our old selves and put on our new selves. Jacob could never have received the family blessing if he hadn't got up from his old life and realised that there was much more on offer.

Whenever I go out and buy a new jumper or pair of jeans, I can't wait to get home and put them on. I am unable to wait until the following day or sometime special to wear the items. Why dress in old dirty clothes when you have a nice new outfit?

Jacob had to actively put down his old life and put on his brother's and then go and stand in his father's presence. Jacob couldn't have just stood behind Isaac and reached out for a bit of a blessing when Esau was being blessed, it wouldn't have worked. Sometimes we take blessings from our heavenly Father like they're those little samples at the supermarket's deli counter. We take a little bit and then go back for more if the product's good. But we learn from Jacob that we need to stand before our Father and take all the good things God wants to give us.

STANDING IN THE HOLY PLACE

In the Psalms the writer says

> Who may ascend the hill of the YHVH?
> Who may stand in his holy place?
> He who has clean hands and a pure heart,
> who does not lift up his soul to an idol
> or swear by what is false.

> He will receive blessing from YHVH
> and vindication from God his Saviour (Ps. 24:3–5).

There is a generation of people who claim to be followers of Christ, yet have no interest in climbing the hill of the Lord and standing in the holy place with him. We've somehow missed the point. For many, Christianity has become a religion of rules and laws, the very thing Jesus came to set us free from. We've made it about performance, about being 'good' enough to stand in his presence. Too often we give up on seeking the hill of the Lord and get settled in the valley of dry bones, trapped in rules and regulations.

The writer of this psalm recognises that only those who are pure and have clean hands will be the ones who receive blessing from the Almighty Father. We are unworthy of this blessing, this gift, because of the sinful nature of our lives. We will never be good enough. But when we are clothed in Christ, we can ascend the hill of the Lord and stand in his holy place.

HE HEARS THE VOICE OF A LIAR

For many years I was content with the valley at the bottom of the hill. Sometimes, I saw people coming down from the hill, their faces shining with his blessing. Sometimes, just hearing their stories and seeing how they'd changed quenched my thirst but I still wanted more.

When I first experienced God's blessing I was fifteen on a Christian camping holiday. I was sat in a damp tent with a few friends and I closed my eyes and said 'Enough's enough, there must be more to this and I want out.' Even though I was in a tent with others it was like

I was standing in the throne room before my Father with him asking me to come towards him. God recognised my voice, that of a sinner but just as he drew me closer, he recognised the clothes of Jesus and so poured out his blessing on me. At that moment I remembered all the things I had done to offend him, but all those things seemed to mean nothing to him. For me his blessing looked like joy, love and self-control all wrapped up together. I was so relieved that the things I had done wrong were gone and I now had a new life to lead. I now knew who I was created to be, I had confidence to come to my Father, trust him and spend time with him. We will look at what this looks like on the ground in later chapters.

God hears the voice of liars, thieves, adulterers and blasphemers. He hears the voice of the greedy, the angry, those filled with lust. He cries out 'Come here, let me touch you, let me smell you,' and then he blesses us as his favoured child. This is the amazing thing about God's love. Anyone can receive the family blessing and anyone can be anointed by the Father, all they need to do is reach out and accept the clothes of the older brother, Jesus.

It is only when we have accepted forgiveness and placed ourselves in Christ that we can receive God's blessing and be made holy. Holiness starts the moment you accept the clothing found in Christ's wardrobe, when you place yourself in his person. Paul writes that 'you were washed, you were sanctified, you were justified in the name of the Lord Jesus Christ and by the Spirit of our God' (1 Cor. 6:11).

In that moment, when you strip down and place on Christ's clothing, all our sins, mistakes and imperfections are no longer of any consequence. For that moment, we are holy and nothing is separating us from the blessing of the Father. For that moment, we are free from everything that holds us back and tells us that we are not children of God. For that moment, we are totally pure. The only danger is that this moment seems to end too soon and we find ourselves orientating ourselves away from the blessing. It isn't God who stopped blessing: it is us who have drawn away.

LIVING IT OUT

- What was your understanding of holiness in the past?

- How has this chapter started to redefine it for you?

- How do you think God sees you? As a liar or as his son or daughter? How does the concept of being a child of God affect you?

- Have there been times in your Christian faith where someone has helped you revise your view of an aspect of God? How was this process helpful?

- Have you ever seen yourself as totally pure after confessing all the things that have blocked your relationship with God? Why not for a moment spend some time writing down everything you have done to offend God? Don't try and over-analyse your life, go with the first things which come into your head, and then prayerfully destroy the list.

  In the act of confession we need to make sure that when God forgives us, we too forgive ourselves.

- You might find it helpful to take the verse from 1 Corinthians 6:11 and spend some time putting yourself in the text – take out the 'you' and put in your name. Read it over a few times and let it sink in.

  '[Your name] is washed, [your name] is sanctified, [your name] is justified in the name of the Lord Jesus Christ and by the Spirit of our God.'

FURTHER READING

The Pursuit of Holiness by Jerry Bridges is a great book investigating and defining holy living. This book is practical and relevant to how we live out a radical holiness.

MISSING THE
SUNSET | 02

THAT LONG TRIP

Some time ago, when I was still living at home, my brother and I decided to take a short trip to our nearest 24-hour supermarket. Fancying a night of junk food and films, we borrowed Dad's car and set off. Chatting all the way about the crisps, cake and fizzy drinks we were going to pig out on, we arrived at the shop in no time and filled our trolley with a ridiculous amount of food. Piling it all in the car, we headed home to begin our movie marathon. We'd done the trip hundreds of times with our parents but never really paid much attention to the ride home. Finding our way there had been easy, but, driving back in the dark on our own, suddenly we weren't as sure of the way. Approaching a junction and needing to make a quick decision about which route to take, we turned right. About forty minutes later, having seen no familiar signs, we decided to do a left turn in the hope that it'd counteract our original right turn. It didn't.

So, feeling a little panicked, we decided to stop at a petrol station for directions. I got out of the car and joined a queue of what looked like four ex-convicts, all of whom appeared to be discussing how one of them had broken someone's arm the night before. Seriously freaked out, I stared at the floor intently until it was my turn to be served by the fresh-faced petrol attendant behind the little glass window. It wasn't good news; we were about an hour's drive away from home, which meant the return trip from the supermarket took almost two hours in total. Starting out with the best of intentions, we'd managed to get ourselves completely confused and a long way from home.

I've come to think that this is a little like holiness. We sometimes find ourselves a long way from our Father and his blessing when all we wanted was to take a twenty-minute trip to the local superstore for some chocolate fudge cake. We set off on the Christian journey thinking we know where we are going, but all to often our attention wanders, we make some silly decisions and find ourselves quite a way from God, with no real idea of how we got there or how to get back. Holiness is all about where we are in relation to God and as we move away from that place of favour and blessing we end up getting lost in the dark landscape. Unholiness is essentially being away from God's blessing and losing your direction, which we will look at further.

OVER THE HILL

Only a few weeks ago, members of my church decided to have a night of prayer. Locking ourselves in the building we spent the night praying and worshipping. It was an incredible time and we saw God moving in crazy ways. But by 6 a.m. we were feeling slightly prayed out and in desperate need of some fresh air. We decided to walk up a nearby hill to see the sun come up over London. So, over thirty young people sat chatting on the hillside, waiting for the sun to rise over the dark city. We must have been there for around fifty minutes before we realised it was getting light even though we couldn't see the sun coming up.

In our sleepy state, we'd all sat facing the wrong direction; the sun had come up behind us whilst we'd been discussing the events of the night. Caught up in the excitement of seeing the sunrise, we'd forgotten to pay attention to its location.

Orientation is so important. What's the point in going to the cinema and facing the wrong way? Surely the film is the main event, the thing you paid to see? Facing the wrong way means you miss out. We all know this, yet some of us Christians spend our life facing away from God, even though we know him well. We get distracted by other things and look away from the most important and most beautiful thing of all, God.

Many of us behave as though God lives on some distant planet, only popping down to earth for odd visits when he has a bank holiday or time to take a break. We act like God is outside of everything we know and understand to be in the world. Almost like an artist who stands back from his painting to admire his work and then comes close to see the detail now and again . . .

THE BUSH WAS ALWAYS BURNING

Nowhere in Scripture do we see a distant God, rather we find the perspective that God is so close everything is therefore spiritual. Almost like God is background noise to everything around us. In the story of Moses and the burning bush we almost get the idea that for the conversation the bush was burning but then stopped when it was over. But what about thinking about it in terms that maybe everything is burning with God's holiness. For that moment God allowed Moses to see how holy the bush was. Almost like Moses was allowed to see how close God really is.

In the book of Exodus it says

> When YHVH saw that he had gone over to look, God called to him from within the bush, "Moses! Moses!"
> And Moses said, "Here I am."
>
> "Do not come any closer," God said. "Take off your sandals, for the place where you are standing is holy

ground." Then he said, "I am the God of your father, the God of Abraham, the God of Isaac and the God of Jacob." At this, Moses hid his face, because he was afraid to look at God. (3:4)

In one of the endnotes earlier we began looking at the idea held by many Jewish believers that everything is sacred, everything is holy.[6] There is no concept of secular work and church work because everything we do is in God's tune within his creation. The idea is that God is 'playing a tune' in and amongst every living cell and atom of the universe. It is almost like God is daily calling out, 'I am the God of creation and history, the God of Abraham, the God of Isaac and the God of Jacob' to the world around us.

Imagine God burning around you all the time just like the burning bush. Almost like a song playing or flames burning in the very cells that make up who you are, burning and beating in the ground on which you stand. Burning and Beating. Burning and Beating. Can you hear the beat; can you sense his holy burning?

The question for Jewish scholars for thousands of years was never 'Is there a God?' or 'Does he exist?' But rather 'Are you aware of his burning? Are you in tune with God's song?'

BEING IN TUNE

Being in a place of holiness is essentially being in tune with God. It's like the human race in a grand cosmic orchestra playing the tune which has been playing since the beginning of time. This isn't lift music, this is the type of tune that when you hear it you can't help but dance. All we need to do is play along with it. Being in the Father's blessing is about playing in tune with his music. We all come across people who claim to be followers of God and talk as if they know everything about him, yet they seem to be way out of tune with his song. The strange thing is, there are those who don't know much about the Father but seem to be really in tune with the song. We need to realise that this cosmic tune is the heartbeat of God holding everything together. Holiness is about being in tune with the Father. It's about orientating ourselves so we can see him, so we can hear his song and know his blessing.

When I was fifteen, I was asked to play in my church's worship band. The rest of the band were much older than me and several of them were professional musicians, so I was really eager to impress them. One evening, when practising with the band, the piano player stopped halfway through a song and turned round to face me. In front of the whole group, he informed me that I was playing completely out of time with the rest. I was mortified and more than a little indignant – I thought my guitar fills were sounding pretty good.

Unfortunately, I was hugely out of time but I just hadn't realised. According to the band, I had slowly gone out of time after the first verse. Heartbroken, I went home that night telling myself I'd never play with them again.

Are you playing out of tune with the cosmic song? Have you ever thought about it before? Could it be that you are so caught up with playing that you haven't thought about getting in time with the song? Could it be that you started bang on time, but because you are playing in a slightly different tempo you're racing ahead – or falling behind?

A week later, I went back to the band practice. I swallowed my pride and listened carefully, making sure I was exactly in time with everyone else. It felt good when I was playing in time and in tune with the others. It's the same with living to God's beat. When we're in time with him, it just sounds better because that's what we were designed to do. When we live with our eyes orientated to him and in time with his heart, we live in a place of blessing.

BEING OUT OF TUNE

In the eleventh chapter of 2 Samuel we see what happened when one of God's chosen leaders became out of time with God.

One night, King David couldn't sleep, so getting up from his bed, he went for a walk on the roof of his palace. From high up on his roof, he saw a woman having a bath – she was very beautiful and David wanted her.

David was a real man of God. He'd followed all of God's directions until then, knowing how to turn his face towards God and live in tune with him. But that night, something else caught David's eye and he chose to walk towards it. He could have realised it was a woman bathing, closed his eyes straightaway, gone back inside, repented over what he saw and decided to watch TV. Instead, he allowed lust to take over and he summoned one of his servants and sent them to invite the beautiful woman back to his place. He chose to orientate himself away from God and towards something else. He chose to do something out of tune with God's song.

What began as just a slight turn away from God, spying on a naked woman, finished with David a long way from home. My wrong turn on the way back from the superstore lead to many more wrong turns, resulting in me being hours away from where I wanted to be. In the same way, David's choice to ignore God led him far from the place of God's favour and blessing. What started as a small disobedience results in adultery, murder and distance from God when David ended up having the woman's husband killed. So many times, I've found myself thinking about whether it's possible to deviate a little from God's blessing. I've wanted to be far away enough to do what I want but still close enough to run back when it all goes wrong. An example of this is when we ask God how many alcoholic drinks we can get away with having or how far we can go with a girlfriend sexually. More and more, I've seen that these are the wrong questions to ask. Rather than asking 'What can we get away with?' we need to be asking:

How can I honour my Father the best in this situation?

What would he want from me in this situation?

How can I become more like him in this situation?

I don't know about you but I tend to forget too often that everything away from the place of God's blessing is unhelpful, damaging and will inevitably distance us from him.

THEY WERE GIVEN OVER

In the book of Romans, Paul writes about a group of people that had orientated themselves away from the place of God's favour.

> For although they knew God, they neither glorified him as God nor gave thanks to him, but their thinking became futile and their foolish hearts were darkened. Although they claimed to be wise, they became fools

and exchanged the glory of the immortal God for images made to look like mortal man and birds and animals and reptiles.

Therefore, God gave them over in the sinful desires of their hearts to sexual impurity for the degrading of their bodies with one another. They exchanged the truth of God for a lie, and worshipped and served created things rather than the Creator—who is forever praised. Amen. Because of this, God gave them over to shameful lusts. Even their women exchanged natural relations for unnatural ones. In the same way the men also abandoned natural relations with women and were inflamed with lust for one another. Men committed indecent acts with other men and received in themselves the due penalty for their perversion (Rom. 1:21–27).

Paul later goes on to say that

They have become filled with every kind of wickedness, evil, greed and depravity. They are full of envy, murder, strife, deceit and malice. They are gossips, slanderers, God-haters, insolent, arrogant and boastful; they invent ways of doing evil; they disobey their parents; they are senseless, faithless, heartless, ruthless (Rom. 1:29).

This passage from Romans speaks of a group of people who had been in the Father's blessing, who had seen the sunset but chosen to orientate themselves away from it. They chose to swap what they knew about God and his holiness for something else. They became out of time with God's tune. They shifted themselves towards every kind of evil and even created new things to take God's place, new sins. The idea of people coming up with new sins always makes me smile because I picture loads of people crammed around a table, with a big pad of paper, designing sins like you would a new drinks can. This sort of orientation is not accidental, it's considered and intentional.

WE DISTANCE OURSELVES

There are so many things we can choose to direct ourselves towards, things we can choose to allow our eyes to glance upon, even though we know the beauty of being in that place of holiness. As we put that distance between ourselves and God, our purity and holiness gets all messed up by our sin.

Sin is essentially anything that is out of God's blessing. I don't always find the word sin helpful because it just makes people think of long sermons and street preachers shouting about hell. Instead, I understand the nature of sin by comparing it to Marmite, which in my house is called 'devil poo juice'. Nothing illustrates sin as profoundly as that dark, evil sandwich topping. Devil poo juice has all the characteristics of sin: it smells foul; it makes people feel sick; it stains and it's sticky. It has an effect on other people when they smell it on you and once you have it on your hands, it marks everything you touch.

Not long ago, I was speaking at a church about how sin affects our lives and I decided to use devil poo juice as an illustration. I wore a white T-shirt and as I named different sins, I smeared the sticky stuff over my nice, clean T-shirt. In less than a minute I was covered. I then demonstrated how our sin affects other people by hugging a guy from the congregation, leaving a gooey mess on his shirt where it'd touched the devil poo juice that I was covered in. I then went off and reappeared in a fresh white T-shirt, representing the purity we find in Christ. The congregation seemed to like it and despite a bit of a fuss about the Marmite I'd dripped on the floor, the whole thing seemed to go well. However, it wasn't until I got home that I actually started to understand my illustration fully. As I got changed, I realised that the devil poo juice had more staying power than I'd previously thought. Under the clean T-shirt, my chest was stained brown, as were my hands and arms. I then found it in my hair. Even after changing out of the clothes and washing thoroughly, I could still smell the stuff on my skin.

I guess we don't always realise how much sin does this. Even the smallest amount leaves a smell around us. Sin affects our lives, the people around us and the relationship we have with God.

This is how I feel so often about my faith and I know others around me do too. We try to present ourselves as sorted and perfect, hiding away what's really inside us. We try to fool people by putting a clean white T-shirt on over the Marmite but then we judge those who have their stains showing. In the Bible it says that when Adam and Eve ate the apple they realised they had things to hide so covered themselves with fig leaves. So many Christians turn up to church on a Sunday morning wearing their fig-leaf outfits acting like everything is sorted, but there's more to being a Christian than looking like we have it all sewn up.

John writes about this Christian attitude to the world around us.

> Do not love the world or anything in the world. If anyone loves the world, the love of the Father is not in him. For everything in the world—the cravings of sinful man, the lust of his eyes and the boasting of what he has and

does—comes not from the Father but from the world. The world and its desires pass away, but the man who does the will of God lives forever (1 Jn. 2:15-17).

It's clear from this passage that we need to be orientated to the Father rather than the world around us but perhaps Christians have misinterpreted what this means. Worldliness, in this passage, seems to go much deeper than the contemporary evangelical idea of worldliness. It's much deeper than the things people see us do. We can avoid 18-rated films, drunken parties and sex outside of marriage but still be jealous, hate people and be proud.

We can be cigarette-free, but untruthful.

Sexually pure but a total gossip.

Modest in dress but greedy in heart.

WHERE OUR HEART IS

Worldliness is about where our heart is. We can live an outwardly perfect Christian life but still have our heart rooted in worldly things like possessiveness, jealousy, pride and snobbery. We can follow all the rules of the Bible but use them to judge and condemn others. We can be wrapped up beautifully and neatly on the outside but still be full of messy things inside. In the gospel of Luke Jesus told a story to help us understand this concept.

There were once two brothers who lived with their father on a successful farm. One of the brothers asked his dad for his inheritance early so he could leave the farm and live a wild life. He blew all his money on drink, sex and buying himself friends. Soon he found himself without a penny. He got a job feeding pigs and realised that even the pigs had better food than he did. So he decided to go home and beg for a job as a servant in his father's house, thinking his dad would be so cross with him he wouldn't want him home. But before he had even arrived his father raced to meet him. He then threw a huge party for him; but the brother that had stayed at home wasn't too pleased. He'd stayed at home to serve his dad, working hard and not living the wild life. He was committed to his family, worked conscientiously and would have been seen as a good Jewish son. He confronted his father with his unhappiness

> Look! All these years I've been slaving for you and never disobeyed your orders. Yet you never gave me even a young goat so I could celebrate with my friends. But when this son of yours who has squandered your property with prostitutes comes home, you kill the fattened calf for him! (Lk. 15:28–32)

The son was living an outwardly moral life, working hard and doing all the things he should. He avoided worldly pleasures yet still had an attitude well out of line. Holiness is not only about trying to emulate a lifestyle that is within the blessing seen in Psalm 24, it's about having the same values as God, not as a set of written rules but as something important to us that's integrated into our hearts. Holiness is about having a heart that plays in tune with our Father's wherever we are.

CORINTH

Sometimes it seems like the only way to live this holy lifestyle is to shut ourselves away from the world, huddled in churches and surrounded solely by Christian friends. At times I have heard people say 'Those people in the Bible had it easy, their culture just wasn't as immoral as ours is today.' The reality was that the early Christians had it just as hard as we do.

Paul wrote strong letters to the church in Corinth calling them away from the world of which they were a part. Corinth was very close to the intellectual centre of Athens and its inhabitants were proud of their lives of luxury and comfort. Corinthians were wealthy, educated, loved sport and wanted entertainment 24/7 – but were mostly known for wild parties, heavy drinking, gluttonous eating and sexual freedom. The famous temple of Aphrodite (who was the goddess of love, lust and beauty) had around one thousand temple prostitutes, all calling men and women in to feast on their sexual desires.

The lifestyle of partying and pleasure seeking was so well known that Romans had a phrase 'to live like a Corinthian'. Corinth was a mess and looked very much like our society. The new Christians Paul wrote to in his letters had it tough.

SANCTIFY

Jesus taught that it was possible to live in this kind of messy world, surrounded by evil things, yet still orientating our hearts to the Father.

Jesus on one occasion prays for his disciples saying 'They are not of the world, even as I am not of it. Sanctify them by the truth; your word is truth' (Jn. 17:16–17).

Jesus uses the word *hagiazo*: in English this is 'to sanctify' which means 'to be set apart'. Holiness is about being in the world but being set apart from the things, which go on within it. When something is set apart, it's usually put to one side so that it is protected or saved for something else. When we put money to one side for a rainy day, we are placing it in a special place where it will be safe. Jesus is calling us to do the same with our hearts, to set them apart from the evil of the world and orientate them towards the blessing of the Father.

Just like David did many years ago, we often set our heart towards things we shouldn't, things that are definitely of this world and not of God's. Or we set ourselves away from the world and call this holiness. But, holiness is more than that. David's mistake wasn't standing at the top of his palace and surveying the world, it was allowing his heart to face away from God. We are called to stand on the rooftops, looking out over our towns and being part of the world we're in. But, we're also called to make sure our hearts are turned towards our Father so that we are in tune with his song and his direction. David's decision to invite Bathsheba back to his place was an outward sign of his heart's orientation. Our challenge is to be 'in the world but not of it' (Jn. 17:14–15), placed in the world but orientated away from it and towards God.

LIVING IN NOT OUT

So many Christians think of holiness as living separately from the world and trying not to break any of the rules in the Bible. But true holiness is about living in the world whilst still living in tune with the Father's heartbeat. It's about being aware of who we present on the outside, but at the same time, who is really on the outside. It's not about rules or our performance: it's about our position.

LIVING IT OUT

- When in your life have you missed God because you were looking in the opposite direction? What things drew your eyes away from him?

- What do you think of the idea that everything is burning like the bush in the Exodus story? Can you see how this affects how you see the world around you?

- What do you think being orientated to God looks like in practice?

- What questions does this chapter leave you with regard to orientation? Is there someone with whom you could work through these questions?

- Worldliness is about where our heart is. Where do you think your heart is right now?

- Where do you want to see your heart in six months' time?

- Is there a way of making sure you put things in place to change your heart?

- Why not spend some time studying these Bible texts and praying about what you want to change in your life?
  Ephesians 2:1–22

  1 Thessalonians 4:1–12

- In what ways are you neatly wrapped on the outside, but living in a worldly way on the inside?

FURTHER READING

Encounters with God by Peter Hicks looks at how people in the Bible are transformed by God when they experience him first hand. It can be used as a devotional and is an enlightening read that will help you tune yourself into God and his big story.

DADDY |03

MY DAD IS . . .

'My dad is better than yours. My dad can build me a go-kart.'

'So what? My dad doesn't need to build me one, he just buys me one.'

'Well, my dad can get me whatever he wants to.'

'My dad's better than your dad because my dad is bigger than your dad.'

'Yeah? My dad could have your dad because my dad's stronger than your dad.'

'Well, my dad could arrest your dad.'

'My dad could knock your dad out!'

Maybe it was just me and where I grew up but those conversations always happened when it was indoor play. Kids often seemed to argue over whose dad was the best. I remember how important dads were for us lads in playground fights; it was almost as though our dads were our own personal Top Trumps card.

Strength	90 per cent
Height	5'11"
Weight	14 stone
Special Gift	(Woodwork) 88 per cent
Fight Ability	63 per cent
Awesomeness	100 per cent

For a while, I was bullied by a gang of lads, mainly because I was unimpressed by sport. P.E. was never my favourite lesson of the week and I would try to avoid it whenever I could. One week I found myself trapped at the bottom of a large rugby scrum. The boys all jumped on me, not because I had the ball, but because they thought it was funny when I got bruised and muddy.

They waited for me after school that afternoon and I had to run all the way home so they didn't catch me. Sometimes, I walked the long way round so I wouldn't have to deal with being at the bottom of a rugby scrum again.

Later that week, I popped into town to get some bits and pieces from the supermarket with my dad. We were chatting away when I suddenly stopped in my tracks: the lads from school were outside the supermarket entrance. I didn't say anything and carried on walking. I was worried they'd see me and make trouble. But, more than that, I was worried about what Dad would say if he saw the boys start on me. I didn't want him to know there was a problem.

Walking close to Dad, I followed him past the group of lads. They all saw me but they didn't say anything, in fact they all looked the other way! I was safe simply because my dad was there. They couldn't touch me because they knew my dad was bigger than them. He was my secret weapon.

LIKE FATHER, LIKE SON

I love the mentality we have as children: 'My dad's with me so I can do anything.'

No bully can get you when he's around; your dad is your own personal bodyguard. Walking into that supermarket was an amazing feeling, I knew that the boys couldn't do anything to me. I felt safe.

I can remember other times that my dad made me feel safe. If I fell over when I was playing, he would pick me up and clean up my grazes. If I came home after wrecking my bike by accident, he would straighten out the wheels and fix it for me. Sometimes, Dad would arrive with a present for my brother and I as a surprise, or build things with us in the garden. I knew that he wanted to look after me and give me good things.

Now I have a little boy of my own and it's made me aware of how important my dad is to me. Looking back, I realise that who I am now was shaped by the way Dad was with me when I was growing up. I do things with my little boy that my dad did with me, playing some of the same games and saying some of the things my dad said to me. The way he treated me, related to me and talked to me, had a direct effect on the way I now view myself. And the way I think about him also affects the way I think about myself. Our upbringing can shape what we think is right or wrong, how we react to stress, and other behaviour patterns. This is true of our relationship with our fathers and our mothers. Both can have a huge effect on our lives and are instrumental in shaping our identity. What I am describing about dads can just as easily be applied to mums.

THIS IS MY SON

Have you ever thought about this with regards to Jesus? If we recognise that our identity is caught up with how we view our dad, then since Jesus was completely 100 per cent man, as well as being completely 100 per cent God, he would have felt and reacted the same way as us. Jesus would have received his identity from God, his father.

There is a story written by Matthew that will help us think through this further. Jesus had a cousin who looked a bit like a hippy. John lived in the desert and smelt like it. He appeared wild, with unkempt hair, and no personal hygiene, but he was desperate to prepare the Jewish people for the arrival of the coming Saviour. Jesus came to John to be baptised in the same way as other people who believed in the message John was preaching. John recognised that Jesus was the person he was waiting for and was more than a little confused about why his Saviour needed to be dunked – but since Jesus insisted he agreed.

As soon as Jesus was baptised, the heavens were opened and everyone saw the Spirit of God descending like a dove on him. Then, the voice of God said 'This is my Son, whom I love; with him I am well pleased' (Mt. 3:17).

To understand this story properly we need to know a few things about the Jewish culture of the time. Jesus was brought up in the family business as many Jewish boys of that time were. A young boy would be trained by his father until they were about twenty or so – then they would start to be able to do some things on their own. But it wasn't until around their thirtieth birthdays when they would fully take over the family business.

At the age of thirty, the son and his father would go to a public place like the market square and the father would stand up and shout in front of the crowd, 'This is my son whom I love, and I am really proud of him.' It was a way of demonstrating to the community that the father loved his son and recognised him as a man who was now old enough to take over the family business. Much of a Jewish boy's identity came from his father publicly declaring his love for him.

This is what was happening to Jesus; his real dad was showing the world how much he loved his son, and handing on the family business. Jesus finds himself publicly being affirmed by God. One version of the Bible translates the Greek as, 'This is my dearly loved son, who brings me great joy.'[7] Imagine how Jesus felt that day, knowing his father not only dearly loved him but that he filled his father's heart with great joy.

This public declaration from the Father was as much for Jesus' benefit as for the onlookers. This was the start of Jesus' ministry, the beginning of him taking over the family business and running it for himself. Jesus was dearly loved and filled his Father's heart with much joy before he had even started his ministry.

Jesus was loved by his Father before he had done or said anything. As we discussed in the earlier chapter, since we are clothed in Christ and stand before God within him, we too are treated as sons and daughters of the Father. Since Jesus was affirmed before he had done anything, the same applies for us. This means that, like Jesus, we don't need to accomplish anything to be loved by our Father. We fill his heart with joy by just coming before him.

> You are his Son and Daughter,
> You are loved,
> You bring him joy.

> You are his Son and Daughter,
> You are loved,
> You bring him joy.

THAT MONKEY THAT CHANGED EVERYTHING

The sad thing is that many of us don't act as though we believe this is true.

There's a small fishing town on the east coast of the UK called Whitby. Whitby is a great place, with boats and sand and all the sights of a northern seaside town. A couple of years ago, some friends and I were hanging out there, taking in the sights and enjoying the fresh fish. We looked at all the normal things like tacky shops and Punch and Judy but there was one attraction we'd never seen before. A small monkey stood on a painted wooden box, with cymbals on his hands, dancing while a scruffy man played an accordion. He was an organ grinder with his monkey. The faster the man played, the faster the monkey danced. I stood watching the monkey with my friends who thought this was a wonderful sight and started chanting 'Dance, monkey, dance'. The more the monkey danced, the more my friends chanted, and the more the monkey skipped about on the small box. Faster and faster the monkey tapped its feet to the music until the old man finished the tune.

Many of us act as though we are a monkey. If I could just perform that little bit better maybe those watching will like me more, maybe I will win the approval of the others, maybe God will be pleased with me.

Dance, monkey, dance.

How often do we act as though that's what we think God is like? People have strange images of God; I once read a book that claimed God was bored with the universe he created so he now runs a small quaint bookshop in South London.[8] Others see God as being like the wizard in *The Wizard of Oz*, sat behind a large screen directing things in the universe, pulling levers and turning cogs. Others see God as someone to impress, someone we need to prove ourselves to: God as the organ grinder.

We believe that in order to gain God's love, his acceptance, we need to pray, to read our Bibles, to do 'good works', to fast, to convert the lost . . . and the list goes on. Don't get me wrong all those are great things to do, but nowhere does it say that God will only love us if we do those things.

ASATAN

Why is it that we feel we need to earn God's love? Where does this urge to be a dancing monkey come from? This performance mentality that tells us that if we pray longer, if we read Scripture more, if we worship that bit harder, if we speak in tongues, if we preach, teach or lead worship, if we heal the sick and move to work with the lepers in Calcutta, then the Father would love us more. In short from Satan.

Satan isn't actually Satan's name; the Hebrew used for what we call Satan is *asatan* or in English, 'the accuser, liar or deceiver'. He really doesn't have a name other than the one who accuses and lies.

The deceiver knows that our identity should come from our heavenly Father. If he can convince us that God is not good and cannot be trusted, then his work with us is pretty much done; we'll move further and further away from our Father. We see this in the story of Adam and Eve in the Garden of Eden when it says that the deceiver, in the form of a snake, persuaded Eve that God had lied to them.

Knowing that God had already spoken to Adam and Eve about the tree of knowledge, he set out to undermine what had been said.

> He said to the woman "Did God really say, 'You must not eat from any tree in the garden'?" The woman said to the serpent, "We may eat fruit from the trees in the garden, but God did say, 'You must not eat fruit from the tree that is in the middle of the garden, and you must not touch it, or you will die.'"
>
> "You will not surely die," the snake said to the woman. "For God knows that when you eat of it your eyes will be opened, and you will be like God, knowing good and evil"(Gen. 3:1–5).

The snake knew that God was good and wants to protect his children, but he wanted Eve to think that God was deceiving his creation and that he didn't want the best for his children. The snake tried to undermine God's love for his daughter, Eve, by telling her that God was hiding good things from her. Satan knows that challenging God's goodness chips away at the very identity we have in Christ. It weakens our sense of who we are and what we are called to be.

Eve looked at the fruit of the tree and thought it looked good. She no longer saw herself as the daughter of the One who cares for us, she wanted knowledge and independence from him. So, she ate the fruit and so did her husband. Then 'the eyes of both of them were opened, and they realised that they were naked so they hid.'

When we listen to the lies the world and Satan tells about ourselves and God, we forget that he loves us naked – faults and all, and think that he will only love us if we are 'good' enough. We become like those performing monkeys – working so hard for acceptance and love that we already have. Instead of knowing that we are sons and daughters of our heavenly Father, we act like servants, or even slaves, of a hard master.

WHAT WE ARE DESIGNED FOR

A while ago, a friend gave my wife and I a present. When we opened the package, it was a small metal implement. We had no idea what it was or what it did. Because I couldn't work it out, I didn't do anything with it and I just stuffed it in a drawer. If we don't know what something is or what it does, how can we expect to know how it works? Objects only reach their potential when they are used for that which they were designed – and that means knowing the purpose of its design.

In our lives, we need to know who we are before we can fully appreciate what God has in store for us. So who are we? We are sons and daughters of a loving father who is also a King. Too often, Satan deceives us into thinking that we aren't children of the King. And when we don't see ourselves as a prince or a princess, we don't act like one. The metal implement turned out to be a designer bottle opener. As soon as I worked out what it was for, it became really useful.

When we don't fully recognise who we are, we end up longing to be someone else. We want to be like a Christian we know because they seem way holier than us. We wish we were them because they look like they love worship or they speak in tongues or they're a superb preacher. Or maybe you find yourself wishing that you were more like someone that doesn't call themselves a Christian, perhaps they have loads of friends, or they're in a fantastic band, or they have perfect hair. Surely we've missed the point somewhere.

When we get to heaven I'm convinced that God will not say to us, 'Why weren't you like Mother Teresa or St Paul?' I'm convinced he will say 'Why weren't you more like Cris Rogers?' (Obviously God will say your name there.)

THE VALLEY OF ELAH

There's a story that explores our need to recognise our own identity in 1 Samuel 17. In the history of the Jewish people there was a time when their future was very unsure. The Jews held a very important trade route called the Valley of Elah, through which products traded between the coastal ports and eastern cities travelled. Israel had lost so much of their land to a group of people called the Philistines, that this was the last bit of property they had left.

The Philistines were now after this valley too. They were a cultured and educated people who produced huge amounts of olive oil and iron back on the coast, which they were desperate to be able to sell to the east and the Egyptians. The Philistine people also had the upper hand on the battlefield since they possessed technology far beyond the Jews (having weapons and armour whereas the Jews didn't).[9]

The battle lines were drawn, with the Philistines gathered on one side and the Israelites on the other.

The Israelites were scared to death of their enemy, because the Philistines also had a special weapon, a giant called Goliath who was more than nine feet tall. No one wanted to fight Goliath – even Saul, King of Israel.

There are clues in the story to tell us quite how evil Goliath appeared to the Israelites. First we learn that Goliath is wearing a 'scaled breastplate' (1 Sam. 17:5). Rabbis[10] would have understood this as the writer telling the reader that Goliath was wearing the sign of the snake, which after the snake in Genesis is seen as representing Satan. In other words Goliath was wearing a sign of the devil. The Jewish reader would have seen that in the same way we would view a swastika, the Nazis' symbol.

Secondly we are told that Goliath stood at 'Six cubits and a span', that his armour weighed 5000 shekels (with some early Hebrew copies of the Samuel text saying 6000 shekels) and that the iron tip of his rod weighed 600 shekels.

6 cubits, 6000 shekels and 600 shekels . . . 666.

The number seven in Jewish tradition is seen as being a perfect number, with seventy-seven as more perfect and seven hundred and seventy-seven even more perfect, and so on. The number six being one less than seven is seen as being a number associated with the devil. Therefore six is an evil number, sixty-six is more so and six hundred and sixty-six – well, I guess you have got the point. So again with this many sixes the writer is again pointing out his links with the devil.

This evil man, who is against everything God is about, then stood up and shouted to the ranks of Israel, 'Why do you come out and line up for battle? . . . Choose a man and have him come down to me.'

None of Israel would take this guy on, and probably rightly so. Would you do it? I know I wouldn't.

A teenage shepherd called David had left his sheep and come to the battlefield to take his brothers some food. As he was talking to them, Goliath stepped out from the Philistine side and shouted his usual challenge to the Israelite soldiers. Knowing that none of the Israelites were willing to battle it out with the giant, David stepped forward and told King Saul that he'd take Goliath on. King Saul replied, 'You are not able to go out against this Philistine and fight him; you are only a boy' (17:33).

But David said to Saul, 'Your servant has been keeping his father's sheep. When a lion or a bear came and carried off a sheep from the flock, I went after it, struck it and rescued the sheep from its mouth. When it turned on me, I seized it by its hair, struck it and killed it' (17:34–35).

Saul finally agreed and gave his tunic to David to wear. He put a coat of armour and a bronze helmet on the boy. David fastened on his sword over the tunic and tried walking around, but it just wasn't happening: David was too small. David tried to clothe himself as someone else but it didn't work.

Years before this battle, David had been selected by the prophet Samuel to be the next king. David knew his calling and he knew his identity in his heavenly Father. David was called to be king when he was a shepherd boy and so he insisted on going to fight Goliath as a shepherd boy, carrying nothing but five smooth stones, his shepherd's bag and a little sling. David left the Israelite camp scared but secure in his identity.

> As the Philistine moved closer to attack him, David ran quickly towards the battle line to meet him. Reaching into his bag and taking out a stone, he slung it and struck the Philistine on the forehead. The stone sank into his forehead, and he fell face down on the ground (1 Sam. 17:48–49).

David ran into battle knowing who he was, the future king. He was called by God to lead the Israelites and because of this, he knew what to do. He wasn't the tallest or the strongest of his family; in fact if we look back to 1 Samuel 16 and 17 we find that his natural dad, Jesse, and his brothers rejected him. But he didn't need to be like them, or like King Saul, to be accepted and loved and then used by God. David just needed to be like David.

Sometimes we feel rejected by those around us, as though they want us to be something or somebody different. We may even try to adapt to fit in, and become like the dancing monkey. Instead we need to know who we are in God, who he has created us to be, and that we need to do nothing but receive his love.

MATTHEW

Matthew quotes Jesus as saying

> Which of you, if his son asks for bread, will give him a stone? Or if he asks for a fish, will give him a snake? If you, then, though you are evil, know how to give good gifts to your children, how much more will your Father in heaven give good gifts to those who ask him! (Mt. 7:9–11)

Many of us struggle with the true amazing-ness of God our Father simply because our dads haven't been the greatest to us. They have damaged our own identity within the Father because of the stuff they have done, either deliberately or not. Jesus recognises this and describes all of our earthly dads as evil in comparison to the goodness of the heavenly Father. We need to see that God is a perfect dad unlike our human ones. Even really fantastic earthly dads are rubbish in comparison to our heavenly Father.

WHO IS YOUR DADDY?

> My dad is not a taxi driver.
> My dad is not a salesman.
> My dad is not a farmer.
> My dad is not a baker.
> My dad is not unemployed.
> My dad is not a teacher.
> My dad is not a fireman.
> My dad is not a policeman.
> My dad is not a doctor.
> My dad is not a judge.

My dad is not a weatherman.
My dad is not a TV celebrity.

My dad is a King.

Stop, pause for a moment.

Your dad is a King.

Let that sink in.

You are a prince or a princess.

You need to feel like it, you need to act like it, you need to walk like it. You need to realise that this gives you authority. You don't need to dance like the monkey to win or gain approval from the Father. You are his dearly loved child, who brings him great joy.

Let's just go back to the Psalms for a moment.

I will proclaim the decree of YHVH:

He said to me, "You are my [Child];
today I have become your Father.
Ask of me,
and I will make the nations your inheritance,
the ends of the earth your possession.
You will rule them with an iron sceptre;
you will dash them to pieces like pottery" (Ps. 2:7–9).

You are a ruler in God's kingdom, if you ask it of him he will give you kingdoms of your own to rule over. For us kingdoms might be areas of gifting, areas of influence, respect or authority. That's how much God loves you, you bring him joy and he wants to give you good things.

Sometimes we miss the point. John writes, 'God so loved the world that he gave his one and only Son' (Jn. 3:16). The psalmist writes that

> He said to me, "You are my [Child];
> today I have become your Father" (Ps. 2:7).

We stand before God in Jesus, we are his children:

You are his son and daughter,

You are loved,

You bring him great joy.

Be set free by the knowledge that God loves you so much he sent his only son for you. Don't keep dancing like the monkey to try and gain something that you already have. It is impossible for the Father to love you anymore than he already does.

We don't need to be dancing monkeys: we just need to sit in the Father's arms and be loved cherished monkeys, gazing into the face of the one that made us.

LIVING IT OUT

- When in your Christian life have you felt you were a dancing monkey for God trying to win his blessing? What was it that made you realise you don't need to perform for him?

- How has your own relationship with your dad affected the way you see your heavenly dad? Sometimes we need our damaged relationship towards our fathers to be healed before we start to see how much our heavenly Father loves us. If this is an issue for you then try and find someone to talk and pray through the issue with: others can see hope where we sometimes can't.

- Knowing that your dad is King, how does that make you feel?

  How does that then help you respond to your own personal Goliaths?

- On a practical level, how can you start behaving like a son or daughter of the King?

- What are the things that help you to remember who you are and what you were designed for? Try writing down the things that help you and make sure you keep doing them, not because they mean God loves you more, but so that you don't forget who you are in him.

- It is so easy to forget who you are when we focus on what God hasn't done, but it is much easier to remember who you are when we focus more on what he has done. Why not think through the things that God has done in your life and your friends' lives and make sure you focus on them. The word 'remember' comes up time and time again in the Old Testament, it was important for the Jews to remember what God had done for them. Why not do a search for the word remember and spend some time looking at how God wanted his people to remember. A few you could look at are: Deuteronomy 5:15; 7:18; 8:12; 8:18; 15:15; 16:3; 16:12; 24:18; Judges 8:33–34.

FURTHER READING

Abba's Child by Brennan Manning encourages us to freely accept that we are a child of the heavenly Father.

FREEDOM | 04

MY BMX AND THE TEST

I've never understood why people retake exams that they didn't fail in the first place, even if it's to improve their grade slightly.

I remember doing my cycling proficiency test when I was a kid. Each week, my little BMX and I went to the local school to learn the correct way to ride my bike on the open road. I didn't want to do it but I knew it was something that had to be done. After four weeks, a group of us lined up to take the test, wearing our little helmets and riding specially polished bikes. The test was simple; we had to ride round some cones signalling with our arms when we needed to turn.

Lining us up at the end of the playground, the police officer stood calling out the names of all those who'd passed the test. Luckily we'd all passed – but only by the skins of our teeth. I'd only just made the grade but was I bothered? Not at all. I was just happy that I had done it and that I could now put that certificate on my shelf and forget about it until I got my 500-metres swimming badge to take its place.

This attitude was not shared by all of the group; one of the lads was so upset about his low mark that he decided to retake all the lessons and the exam itself. I didn't see the point; why waste perfectly good summer nights just to go back to something you could have left behind? No one I know has ever passed their driving test and decided to take it again, just to get a better mark. What's the point? A pass is a pass; there is no need to walk a path that you have already walked.

ELEUTHERIA

Paul tells us 'It is for freedom that Christ has set us free. Stand firm, then, and do not let yourselves be burdened again by a yoke of slavery' (Gal. 5:1).

In the original Greek, the word that Paul uses to describe what Christ has achieved is *eleutheria*. Above, it is translated as freedom, but it could also be 'liberty' so a number of Bible translations render this verse, 'It is for liberty that Christ has set us free.'

A lecturer once told me that 'liberty' is one of the oldest words in the English language and it means 'being free from restriction or control'. It is the power to act and express ourselves as we want to. It's about being physically and legally free from confinement, servitude or forced labour.

So what's Christ set us free from? It is sin. Sin is a word that is hard to relate to and often we see it as something that only involved Adam and Eve. Standing before the tree in the Garden of Eden the first two humans allowed sin to enter the world by eating the apple (or whatever fruit it really was). When Adam and Eve chose to eat the fruit, Satan had convinced them both that God was not all good and that he was hiding something from them.

Sin, to many of us, is a distant thing that doesn't have any impact in the real word around us. The trouble is that sin didn't just enter the world thousands of years ago but that it enters the world every single day when we choose to pick and eat the apples of greed, lust, anger, pride, jealousy and self-centeredness. This sin then starts to affect all aspects of our lives, it changes the way we see the world and others around us. In an earlier chapter we used the image of devil poo juice to show how sin not only affects us but also those around us. This sin, which we bring into the world then starts to hold us down and becomes almost like a legal contract between Satan and us. He owns us.

Paul used this word eleutheria or 'liberty' to remind his readers of the legal and spiritual ties that bind us to Satan. This is the reason that Christ died on the cross to set us free from this contract, to free us from the debt we owed Satan.

OXEN AND YOKES

Jesus died so that we would be legally set free from our confinement and separation from God. It's like we've got stuck facing away from God and his blessing. The cross frees us from that position so that we can re-orientate ourselves back to him. Paul sees Christ as the liberator, the one who came to set us free from being a slave to our sins. Christ's death is the eternal perfect sacrifice by which every person is liberated from the grip sin has on his or her life.

Paul was also reminding the original readers of his letters that Christ's death sets us free from the ties of the Old Testament Law found in the Torah. The Jewish people found the Law a complete struggle, something they just couldn't achieve. They had even added more laws to explain and enhance the laws that were in the Bible. They had lost the point of the laws, which were meant to be about keeping Israel a holy worshipping people separate from those around them. Instead the rules became the aim and the purpose was to win the favour of God through following the Law exactly. Like the dancing monkey, the Jews felt like they needed to obey so that God would love them and bless them.

If they could just get it right, dance a little faster, jump a little higher, they might be free from their sin. Faster and faster and higher and higher they would dance to try and reach something that was never really achievable. Paul is saying the complete opposite of this: Christ came to free you from the dancing. God has given us freedom of acceptance and freedom of access to him, through Jesus. Paul is reminding the Jewish people that through Christ we are all now free from the Law.

Paul uses the image of an ox being weighed down by the heavy yoke that it is carrying. A yoke is a crossbar with a U-shaped section that encircles the neck of an ox. The yoke would be heavy and would be attached to something even heavier to pull. All of this would cause the ox to be held down and forced to lower itself under the heavy weight. Once the ox is freed and the yoke removed, he is able to stand and be free to move as God intended.

Do you ever feel like that ox? Paul says that we are all under the weight of a yoke that is the law of religion. We are burdened by demands that we can never meet which makes us fearful of the punishment we will receive because of it.

Paul reminds us in his letter to the Galatians that the Father sent his son to be punished so that we might be free from punishment. 'Christ redeemed us from the curse of the law by becoming a curse for us, for it is written: "Cursed is everyone who is hung on a tree"' (Gal. 3:13).

If this is the case and Christ has taken the yoke from our shoulders we should stand up tall and dance and celebrate the fact.

LOVE WINS

So how do we get free from the bondage of sin, law or guilt? How do we ensure the yoke is removed from our shoulders?

Firstly, we need to realise in our heads and our hearts that God is completely good and that he would never lie to us, and to understand that he wants the best for us. We need to ask God to help us search our hearts for sins that maybe we didn't realise we'd committed or things that we didn't realise were sins in the first place. It can be helpful to sit and write these down, naming them as God reveals them to us. Take time and quiet to allow the Holy Spirit to move in you and to hear God speak to you.

It is crucial that we don't get caught up in dwelling on our sins too much. When we gaze upon Christ and his perfect nature, we start to see our own failings and shortcomings. But, instead of staying at that place with our sins, we need to look at God's saving love, because we know love wins and make that our focus.

Secondly, we need to take responsibility for our actions, accepting that they're the result of our choices and no one else's.

Thirdly, we need to come to terms with the fact that liberation and freedom is possible through the cross and that when Christ said 'It is finished' that it actually was and it still is because love wins.

SEAFOOD AT THE WING DRAGON

I love going out for Chinese food with my friends, especially when it's all-you-can-eat buffet. A few years ago, I decided to try some sweet and sour seafood, which didn't end very well. After only a few mouthfuls, I realised that seafood and Cris Rogers do not mix. It really wasn't a nice experience. A couple of months back, I decided to eat some seafood pizza at my friends' house in the States. For some reason, I hadn't learned from my previous encounter with the food of the sea, I felt dodgy for hours.[11]

Humans are pretty rubbish at learning from their mistakes, be it with food or with issues of sin. We always seem to end up going back down a road we'd sworn to keep away from. Paul was thinking about this when he wrote 'stand firm, then, and do not let yourselves be burdened again by a yoke of slavery' (Gal. 5:1). Don't go back to the thing that once held you back.

When we stand before the Father and confess our failings, honestly regretting them and how they have hurt God, we truly turn away from our sins. This is called repentance.

I can think of loads of times when I said the words of confession and tried hard to feel forgiven, when I knew deep down that I wasn't really sorry – I didn't really want to give that sin up. That's not repentance.

TO THINK DIFFERENTLY AFTER

The Hebrew word for repentance is made up of two verbs, *shuv* meaning 'to return to', and *nicham* meaning 'to feel sorrow for'.

We can understand the word 'repentance' by bringing together the two meanings 'returning to' and 'change through sorrow' so that the whole word means, 'to think differently after'. We look back on our sin and change because of it.

This understanding of repentance speaks of a change of mind accompanied by regret and resulting in a change in our actions and thoughts. Together, this means a change of heart and mind.

A good example of this understanding of repentance would be the parable of the two brothers we looked at earlier. The New Testament parable talks of the brother coming to his senses, regretting his actions and returning to his forgiving father.

I started to learn my lesson on forgiveness in my late teens. My brother and I were light-sabre duelling in our parents' back garden when we knocked over a garden ornament and broke it. Not really caring that much about what I'd broken, I said a quick 'Sorry!' to my Dad and carried on fighting. That seemed to be enough for him and the matter was quickly forgotten. A couple of weeks later, it suddenly hit me that my 'Sorry' had been totally meaningless. I had given the sorry no thought or consideration and had simply just blurted it out as a gut reaction with no afterthought. True repentance isn't about saying 'Sorry, Dad' as a knee-jerk reaction: it's about noticing our lack of awareness of others and wanting to change this inside us.

FACES TO THE GROUND

Nehemiah 8 is a fantastic image of true repentance. All the people assembled in a square in the city and a guy called Ezra brought out the book Leviticus, the book of the Law, which God had commanded Israel to follow.

Ezra stood before the gathering of men and women and read aloud from the book from early morning until lunchtime. A lot of people struggle with reading this part of the Bible because they find it boring but Nehemiah says that the people listened.

After many hours of reading, Ezra praised God for the teaching and all the people lifted their hands in response and then bowed down and worshipped YHVH with their faces to the ground.

After the time of worship was over, Nehemiah stood facing his people and said to them, 'This day is sacred to YHVH your God. Do not mourn or weep' (8:9). He said this because the people had been weeping as they listened to the Law and began to realise how they had fallen short of God's plan.

Nehemiah told them to go and enjoy food and drink because that day was sacred to God, saying 'Do not grieve, for the joy of YHVH is your strength.' Nehemiah describes the day of repentance as sacred to God. Have you ever thought about your day of repentance being sacred and holy to God?

That's how the Father sees your confession: sacred.

In this story we see that true repentance involves both tears and laughter.[12] Tears of sorrow for our sin, but also laughter and partying with food and drink because of the freedom found within repentance.

Like Nehemiah, Paul calls us to realise that we are to enjoy the wonderful freedom found in the cross of Christ and that we should not let anything tell us otherwise.

REFUSING TO GO BACK

But, much deeper than simply being set free from sin, Christ has also set us free from the guilt of our sins.

It isn't just the act of sin that ties us up: it's also the act of holding on to our guilt. Often, I come across young people who can't let go of the guilt they feel for sleeping with their boyfriend or girlfriend or getting drunk in the park – even though they have come to Christ and asked for forgiveness. I think this stems from not believing that God can truly forgive or really love us. These feelings do not come from our Father who wants to bless us and tell us that we are his children. They come from the snake that wants to keep us away from God.

When we act like this we are like the boy I mentioned earlier who passed the bike test, but somehow it didn't seem enough, he had to go back again to make sure he had done really well. Sometimes we ask for forgiveness, and we are truly sorry, but we can't quite believe that God's done it. So we go back again and again, feeling guilty and tearing ourselves up about what we did. Whereas God has already forgiven it, dealt with it.

When we stand before God and deeply call out to him for his forgiveness, Jesus is on the cross, calling out 'It is finished.' He's crying out 'It is done, don't tear yourself up over it, don't feel guilty about it. I have sorted it; I have paid the price.'

Some things just aren't as complicated as religious people make them out to be. Imagine being locked up in a cell, with loads of chains tying you down. One chain represents the sin of lying, another, the sin of getting drunk and another, the sin of greed. There is no way that we could ever get free from these chains; we just don't have what it takes to get out of them. John wrote that the key to being set free from these chains of sin is to know the truth of Christ.

'And you shall know the truth, and the truth shall make you free . . . Therefore if the Son makes you free, you shall be free indeed' (Jn. 8:32,36 NKJV).

The knowledge and acceptance of Christ is the only key that will open these chains.

It is important to note that freedom isn't just about knowing that Christ died on the cross. Freedom only comes when we understand and accept this for ourselves, not just as a historical fact. So, we stand up, undo our chains and walk out of the cell and that is the point when we're free, when we're re-orientated to our Father again. It's like we're born all over again. Hmm, that sounds familiar, doesn't it?

It's walking out and not looking back. It's refusing to put the yoke back on.

So you passed the test, you're out of the exam; you don't ever need to go back there again. But we do, don't we? I know so many people that have managed to give up smoking then started again a couple of weeks later. Smoking is so addictive; it's hard to leave it behind completely. It's the same with sin, once sin has a hold on you it has the power to creep back into your life. Sometimes, it feels like we were never really free in the first place because of our sins and the guilt we feel about them.

HOW DO WE NOT FALL BACK?

So, how do we avoid falling back into the need to perform for God's love? Earlier we spent some time looking at how Paul told us to 'stand firm' in Galatians 5:1 – but how do we actually do this? We need to set our sight upon the Father and orientate ourselves towards him.

The other day, I was so hungry that I practically ran into one of the big shops in the shopping centre. I was so desperate to get to the sandwich section that I rushed through the shop, not even noticing the products that lined the aisles around me. I got to the refrigerated food section in no time, picked a sandwich and walked to the queue.

In the queue were several of the young people from church, all waiting to be served. As I started to chat to them, it turned out that they'd seen me on my way into the shop. Apparently they had tried to say hi but I just walked straight past them. Worse than that, I'd nearly knocked one of them over in the hair dye section as I rushed by. How embarrassing! I was so caught up in my mission to find food that I hadn't noticed people around me. How is it possible that I am able to avoid anyone and anything that gets in the way of a chicken and bacon sandwich but I can't manage to avoid things that pull me away from the blessing of my Father?

When we orientate ourselves towards God, stand before him to receive his blessing, looking deeply into his eyes, we can no longer bow our heads to put the yoke back on: we are standing firm.

CLEAN BREAK OR ROAD BACK

Sometimes however, we keep returning to our sins because we haven't made a clean break with our old habits. We have asked for and received forgiveness, we are directed towards the Father, but out of the corner of our eye we keep looking at the thing from which we have been forgiven. We leave ourselves a road back to our old life, just in case. We don't sever a relationship we should; we keep certain things, for example, cigarettes or drugs 'just in case'. We just want to keep our options open.

I was once supporting a guy who was coming off drugs. He was trying really hard and making progress but whenever he felt low, he found himself returning to the things he'd left behind. He didn't cut off his past and so it was all too easy to get hold of some gear when he wanted it.

We need to delete numbers from our mobiles and clear out the secret places in our rooms. We need to block up the road that leads us back.

Acts 19:18–19 says

> Many of those who believed now came and openly confessed their evil deeds. A number who had practiced sorcery brought their scrolls together and burned them publicly. When they calculated the value of the scrolls, the total came to fifty thousand drachmas.

A drachma was a silver coin worth about a day's wages. Would you let go of your past if it would cost you fifty thousand days' pay? That's 136 years' worth of wages. Letting go of our past can and does cost us, in terms of relationships, money and popularity. But isn't freedom worth the cost?

DUMP YOUR FILTH

Sometimes the obscure Bible verses catch our attention in ways that the normal Sunday church readings don't. Within the Torah is the Jews' history and law of their faith. Two books particularly speak about how to live and worship: Leviticus is one and Deuteronomy is the other. There is one specific text in Deuteronomy which speaks to the people on a campsite about how to conduct themselves.

> When you are encamped against your enemies, keep away from everything impure . . . Designate a place outside the camp where you can go to relieve yourself. As part of your equipment have something to dig with, and when you relieve yourself, dig a hole and cover up your excrement. For YHVH your God moves about in your camp to protect   you and to deliver your enemies to you. Your camp must be holy, so that he will not see among you anything indecent and turn away from you (Deut. 23:9,12–14).

In ancient Jewish times God's people would move from place to place in their canvas homes, going to war with the surrounding settlements, representing their God, YHVH. When the sun went down, they would sit around campfires singing praises to YHVH and telling stories of what God had done for their nation and how he had created the world. These campsites would become their home and the fellow campers their family from the time they went to war until they arrived safely home. In reality these camps would become the Jewish people's life, it was all that they knew.

God understood the camp to be a place that was holy and the surrounding area to be unholy. These people represented YHVH and the text says that YHVH chose to move about the camp with his people and expected the camp to have a high level of cleanliness.

God said your camp is holy, so keep it holy. Don't have anything in your camp, which would offend me and make me turn my eyes away from you. Don't have anything in your camp which will damage my relationship with you to the point where I will not be able to protect you from all that the world wants to throw at you.

The message is 'If you need to relieve yourself, don't do it in the place YHVH moves, do it in the place where other gods move.' God said take your shovel, dig a hole and leave your filth there.

In all my life I have never come across anyone who chose to go back to the toilet to have another look at his or her filth. This is why God says go outside the camp and leave your filth behind, coming back into the camp pure and holy. God wanted their filth to be a past event and not a present reality.

Are you starting to realise that this is confession language?

The Bible was obviously given to us in written form but within it there are these wonderful images of how faith works out in practice.

Keep your camp, your life, holy as YHVH is holy so that he can move freely in all that you do. And when you need to dump your filth, those things that you carry which will offend YHVH, go to a place where you can dump your waste and leave it behind. It's a past event so dump it.

What do you have in your camp that offends God? What do you need to dump?

Have you ever found yourself confessing your darkest sins and then, days later, going back over the path you have already trodden and picking up past filth and starting to lug it around all over again?

God says bury it, leave it, and never return.

DEATH BRINGS LIFE IN THE PRESENT TENSE

The reason we can be forgiven of our sins isn't because we have buried anything but because Jesus, who died on the cross, has set us free. The life giving freedom we can have isn't what Jesus did on the cross, but what he does every day on the cross. Every day Jesus is healing us, loving us, caring for us, serving us and setting us free from our guilt. Too often we focus on the bloodiness what happened two thousand years ago and forget what the cross does every moment of the day. The cross was never a one-off event. It isn't in the past tense.

Another part of keeping away from our old sins and focusing on God is tied in with repentance. Remember how the Hebrew word for repentance meant two things, 'returning to' and 'change through sorrow' with the whole word meaning 'to think differently after'? We need to find new ways of thinking differently. In Romans it says that we should no longer 'conform . . . to the pattern of this world, but be transformed by the renewing of [our] minds' (Rom. 12:2). Then later it says that we shouldn't live in our old ways, 'Instead, clothe yourselves with the Lord Jesus Christ, and do not think about how to gratify the desires of the sinful nature' (Rom. 13:14).

FLARES, TRAINERS AND JUMPERS

The only way to renew our minds is to bring about total renewal, both of mind and of our clothing. This does not mean that if you change your dress sense everything will be OK.

Flares to skinny jeans.

Trainers to sandals.

Jumpers to jackets.

But it's exactly like we looked at earlier. If we are wearing the clothing of the other brother, Jesus, we start to live and behave differently.

Daily prayer and Bible reading is essential if we want to renew our minds to be more like Christ. We have to let ourselves be transformed.

Why is it that we find it easy to spend so much time with friends or watching TV, but we are unable to find the time to spend it with God in the renewing of our minds? It means that we need to be disciplined with our time and it requires us to be more determined to meet with the Father, because everything else in the world will demand time of you.

Make it a priority to spend time reading and studying the Bible and meeting with God's presence in prayer each day. There are lots of good books out there on issues of holiness, worship, grace, forgiveness, prayer and so on, but none of them are as powerful as reading the actual words of Jesus in the Bible or hearing him speak to you in a quiet moment. How can anything that is regurgitated theology be as good as the original material?

ONLY THE GOOD THINGS

Finally, we need to feed and fill our minds with the things that are good and holy. This means we need to be more disciplined with what we watch, listen to and read. How can we profess to be holy followers of Christ but during the week listen to music that has so many profanities it sounds like one long BEEEEEEEP? We need to wise up to what we are letting occupy our minds.

Let's be honest for a moment.

If you were to look after a child for a few days what would you watch, listen to and read when they were around? Would you let them watch what you watch? Would you let them listen to what you listen to? In reality, I am far more protective of what I will allow my little boy to watch than I am with my own viewing.

Yet I am making huge decisions about the renewal of my mind every day when I make these decisions.

If we go ahead and stuff our minds with images and words from this world, we will end up conforming to this world without even knowing it.

We need to switch on our renewed minds and fill them with new thoughts. We need to keep away from the thoughts that distanced us from the Father in the first place. We need to think fresh thoughts that are worthy of our changed heart and mind.

LIVING IT OUT

- Have you experienced being free from restriction or control in your own Christian faith? What things were you freed from when you started following Jesus?

- Typically as we become free from one thing we realise that there is another thing holding us down. What things at the moment do you need freeing from?

- Can you see how your behaviour might be holding others down? It could be the way you speak to them or what you say, or maybe your actions. Do you need to do more to help someone experience God's freedom?

- Many of us very rarely look at ourselves enough to see how we oppress people by being overbearing or non-diplomatic. Why not spend some time talking with a friend you can trust about how your actions come across. How do you need to change to give others freedom?

- Through Christ's death we are set free from death and given new life in him. How do you think this new life would practically look in day-to-day living? What behaviour do you think we need to leave behind?

- Spend some time praying over Bible verses about freedom. Think about what your life would be like without this freedom and how you need to experience more freedom in certain areas. Here's a few verses to help: Galatians 5:1; 5:13; 1 Peter 2:16.

FURTHER READING

What's So Amazing about Grace? by Philip Yancey is an excellent book looking at stories of God's freedom found in his grace.

Songs of Freedom edited by Eileen Mitson takes us behind the masks we wear and helps us with issues of self-image, eating disorders, sexual abuse and bullying.

The Discipline of Grace by Jerry Bridges look at grace as the key to enjoying the freedom that is offered by Jesus on the cross.

A HOLY GOD | 05

IT'S ALL IN THE COMPARISON

Sometimes, when I'm with people, I feel like a pretty funny person. I make loads of jokes and witty comments fly all over the place: people even laugh. But next to my brother, who's a comic genius, I sound like the embarrassing uncle of the family. I hate standing alongside sporty people because it makes me notice that I'm slightly bigger than average around the waist area. But I love going into primary schools to do assemblies because I'm always the tallest person in the corridor. There are also times when I'm talking to someone and I'm completely struck by how much cooler or better looking or trendier they are than me. It's only when we stand next to other people that we are able to judge ourselves against them.

I'm not saying this is a good thing but it's definitely the case. How do you know you're taller than someone? You stand next to them and see how you measure up, you make a judgement.

Sports contests only happen because we are willing to judge someone against someone else. Exams only work because they reveal how good we are at something against others.

In the same way, it isn't until we start to see the true holiness of the Father and stand alongside him that we truly see how unholy and imperfect we are.

THE SHEMA

Earlier this year, I was asked to speak at a conference on the topic of the Universal God – about how huge the God of creation is and how that impacts our lives. To prepare for this conference, I did quite a lot of reading and my eyes were slowly opened to a piece of text I had never really known or understood before.

One of the central prayers of the whole Jewish faith is the Shema. The Shema has been prayed for thousands of years and is still prayed today. This prayer is said by Jews twice a day and is taught to a Jewish child from the moment it can speak. Our son's first word was 'Goal!' What does that say about our parenting skills?

Originally, the Shema was made up of only one text, Deuteronomy 6:4, although the prayer itself is split into three parts. We'll only be looking at the first section.

> Hear, O Israel: YHVH our God, YHVH is one. Love YHVH your God with all your heart and with all your soul and with all your strength. These commandments that I give you today are to be upon your hearts. Impress them on your children. Talk about them when you sit at home and when you walk along the road, when you lie down and when you get up. Tie them as symbols on your hands and bind them on your foreheads. Write them on the door-frames of your houses and on your gates (Deut. 6:4–9).

At first glance, this looks like a simple text but actually it's full of important theology that we need to get to grips with if we want to understand more about the God of the universe.

Please, don't get me wrong, I'd read these verses before but I'd never looked at them as Jewish before. Rudely, I'd assumed that the book I held in my hands was a Christian book. What a silly presumption. So much of the Bible is steeped in Jewish understandings, Jewish world views and Jewish concepts. It's basically written in a Jewish context by Jewish people. I come to the Bible with my twenty-first-century goggles and I try to read the text from my perspective and not the perspective of the original writers.

SMELL, LOOK AND TASTE

To truly understand many of the books in the Bible, you need to get past the words written on the page and try and see what is going on behind it. What did the world of the writer look like, smell like, taste like? What is its political and historical context? Who is it written for? What does it aim to do?

Our job is to try to take off our modern glasses and put on glasses that help us to see what is really going on in the text. It's quite hard to do but highly important.

The Bible is written in a foreign language and it needs to be translated, but not just from its original language to English. The situations, the examples, the parables and the phrases all need to be understood in the context they were written so we can wholly understand what they mean for us today. It's like hearing half a telephone conversation and needing to know what the other half is saying to truly make sense of it.

When we understand this, we start to notice things about the Bible that we might have overlooked previously. I never realised before that in Mark's Gospel, when Jesus was asked 'What is the most important commandment?' he quoted the Jewish Shema in answer.

> "The most important one," answered Jesus, "is this: 'Hear, O Israel, the Lord our God, the Lord is one. Love the Lord your God with all your heart and with all your soul and with all your mind and with all your strength'" (Mk. 12:29–30).

In the past, I had understood this passage as Jesus stressing the importance of loving God with our whole hearts and lives and that from this, our love for our neighbours would follow. I hadn't understood the true depth of Jesus' answer until I'd got to grips with the Shema.

It's one of the many examples of Jesus' true Jewishness; Jesus is placing the Shema above any other commands, therefore authorising and agreeing with the teachings of the rabbis of the time who taught that the Shema was the greatest of the commands too. If the Shema is this important to Jesus, we need to understand it fully and work out why it is so central to the Christian faith as well as to the Jewish faith.

ONE

Hear, O Israel: YHVH our God, YHVH is one (Deut. 6:4).

Christians don't spend that much time thinking about God's oneness. We talk a lot about God as trinity but miss the concept of his oneness. Now, don't get me wrong, God revealed himself to us as Father, Son and Holy Spirit and it's vital we acknowledge this. But part of the mystery of the Trinity is that God is three yet one.

YHVH our God is 'one'.

Understanding God's oneness is key to understanding who he is and what he is like. Let's spend a little time trying to understand this oneness.

If God is one, it means he has no division within him and no bits that have been added on. God is complete and pure in every possible way. Therefore, none of his characteristics are incomplete. For example if God is love, he is completely, wholly love. There is nothing about his character that isn't loving. He is 100 per cent love. He is perfect love.

When something is perfect, it is faultless, complete and precise. It has no flaws, no cracks and no marks. It can't be improved in any way. It is just right. God's oneness is faultless, it's complete. His oneness can't be improved in anyway.

When we get to grips with the idea that God is 'one', we start to understand a little more about his nature. For example, if God is 'one', it means there are no other gods. How could there be if God is completely God and he is 'one'? This was hugely important to the Jews because they were surrounded by other religions that claimed that their gods could take down YHVH. The Shema is making it clear that there are no other gods who are able to add or take away from YHVH. Nothing and no one can detract from God because he is 'one'.

If God is one and he is perfect, it means there are no other forces of power that can touch him. Not in our universe. Not outside this universe. We're back to 'My dad's bigger than your dad' again, aren't we? God is untouchable.

If God is untouchable then he is omnipotent. Omnipotent is a great word for describing God, it means someone who has unlimited power and authority.

The implications of God's oneness don't stop there. If God is 'one' then he must also be unchanging. If he is wholly perfect how can he change? If God changed it would mean he was moving closer to or away from perfection. We know that's not possible because God is 100 per cent perfect, he can't be more than or less than this.

God is unchangeable.

Stop for a moment and think about that . . .

God is unchangeable; he is the same today as the day he created the world. He is as powerful today as he was on the day he put the mountains into place; he is still as creative as he was when he called the stars into being.

He never changes. That means he is still able to do miracles. The days of turning water into wine, healing the sick and bringing the dead back to life aren't over. If this is true, why don't we live like these things are still possible? More than that, if God is unchanging it means he wants to do these things today like he did two thousand years ago.

WHAT DOES THAT MEAN FOR US?

He never changes. That means that when we pray he always responds lovingly and with our best interests at heart. Sometimes, it feels like God answers our prayers randomly, depending on whether he's having a good day or not. It feels like we cry out to him and sometimes, when he can be bothered he answers, but other days he just ignores us. But if we think about God's oneness, we know that can't be true. God is always interested in our lives; he always responds to our prayers, he always loves us. That should change the way we pray.

God is nothing like Cris Rogers. I am getting older every day, which I've started to notice more and more. I used to be able to eat more curry than anyone I know but these days I feel a bit dodgy after a big Indian meal. But, it's not just my body that's changing. I'm finding that every day I am becoming more aware of the world around me: my heart is breaking more and more for the poor, the oppressed and the marginalised.

God isn't like that, he isn't changing and his views are still the same. His heart is still broken for the poor, he still wants the best for us, he still loves us with the passion he did on the day he created us and the day he died for us.

God is the same; he is unchanging. That means he doesn't grow and learn like we do. For God to grow and learn he would have to be imperfect to start with and we know that's not true.

GOD DOES NOT DO RESEARCH

If I wanted to find out what the best fish and chip shop in the area was, I'd ask people. I'd get some opinions, I'd make enquiries, and I'd research.

God does not do research as he knows everything.

For God to get new information it would require him to change. The Shema makes it clear that God is one, he is perfect, he is unchanging which means that he is already all-knowing (the word for this is omniscient).

Jesus knew what he was saying when he was approached by the teacher of the law. God is the only God, it is his show, there's no support act.

The Shema leads us to understand that if the Father is good then he is perfectly good. If this is not the case then he would be partly one thing and partly another. Partly just and partly unjust? Partly fair but sometimes unfair? That's not the 'oneness' the Shema describes.

If the Father is loving, he is perfectly loving.

If the Father is caring, he is perfectly caring.

If the Father is merciful, he is perfectly merciful.

If the Father is forgiving, he is perfectly forgiving.

If the Father is generous, he is perfectly generous.

If the Father is perfect, he is perfectly perfect.

LIMITED

All of this made me start thinking about whether God is limited in any way. Is there anything he can't do? Let's start by reading the opening scene of the creation story: 'In the beginning God created the heavens and the earth' (Gen. 1:1).

Imagine God creating everything that is seen and unseen, calling everything around us into being. But imagine this: before creation there was God.

Before creation, God.

Before the world, God.

Before air and sky, God.

Before light and dark, God.

Before anything, God.

Before anything was created there was nothing but God. There wasn't God and a little bit of space for him to stretch out if he got cramp. There wasn't a bit of room to his left. God was all there was. Which means that God was all alone with nothing for company – can you imagine it? Nothing.

TSIMTSUM

If there was nothing other than God, where did God create the universe? Rabbis have been debating this for centuries and come up with the theology of *tsimtsum*. If God is perfect, as the Shema states, the thought is that he couldn't have created the universe within himself because that would have meant changing. Some traditional Jewish thought states that the omnipotent God created a plot of nothingness by withdrawing from a space he usually filled. Then, in this space, God made the universe. The word that is traditionally used for this idea is *tsimtsum*, the act of withdrawing.

David writes at the beginning of Psalm 90 'YHVH, you have been our dwelling-place throughout all generations.' We have in fact been dwelling within him all this time and never known. God is the very dwelling place of the entire universe but we need to remember that this universe is not God's dwelling place.

Although I can buy into God's act of withdrawing I certainly don't buy into the idea of God creating everything in a Godless vacuum, it's just not biblical. We know and believe that God is everywhere, thus making everything sacred. God is different to us, he can be everywhere at all times. But there are also accounts in Scripture of God withdrawing, but they don't mean that there is a God vacuum left, a place where God isn't at all.

Instead God is understood as being distant, but at the same time still in the location. For example we see God enter the tabernacle, or leave the temple, we see him withdrawing from or arriving at a place. For most Jewish rabbis this doesn't meant that God isn't in a location then arrives, but that at times he is more 'concentrated' or his presence is felt more intently than at others. So in that respect he limits himself and his presence.

In the book of Deuteronomy, we find an image of God who walks amongst the Israelite camp (23:14), and at different times he arrives, dwells, wanders but then leaves. The camp in Deuteronomy is never God's home, but the home of the Israelite people, in the same way that this earth is not God's home, it is ours.

GRADED HOLINESS

A Jewish way of seeing the world is that of graded holiness. It's the idea that there are some places that are more holy than others. We would say that a church building was somehow more holy than our toilet and early Jews would say the tabernacle in the Old Testament was more holy than outside the camp where they had their toilet area.

As you are sitting right now reading this book we could say that perhaps God's presence is around you but not intently, perhaps 30 per cent in concentration. But in an act of worship where his Spirit is moving there might be a more intense presence of God, perhaps a concentration of 90 per cent around you. One friend I know thinks of it as a smell or an aroma, sometimes the aroma of God is strong, other times it is faint reminding us that 'He is with us, his spirit is here.'[13]

Moses had the closest relationship with God of everyone in the Bible. So he asked if he could see God's face. However, God told Moses

> ". . . When my glory passes by, I will put you in a cleft in the rock and cover you with my hand until I have passed by. Then I will remove my hand and you will see my back; but my face must not be seen" (Ex. 33:22,23).

The word used here for 'face' is the Hebrew word *paniym* which can also be translated as 'presence'. The same word is seen in the King James translation of Genesis when Adam and Eve 'heard the voice of YHVH walking in the garden in the cool of the day: and Adam and his wife hid themselves from the presence [*paniym*] of YHVH amongst the trees of the garden' (Gen. 3:8).

They hid themselves from his *paniym*, but why? Earlier in Genesis it says that 'The man and his wife were both naked, and they felt no shame' (2:25). The Torah is quick to mention they had no shame in Genesis 2 but when they are kicked out of the garden the immediate effect of their breaking the rules, or eating the fruit, is that they suddenly realise that they are naked. Because of this Adam and Eve fear God, which means that there must be a connection between the acts of knowing we have things to hide, feeling shame and being unable to stand face to face (*paniym* to *paniym*) with God.

So the presence of God around us is limited by the shame we feel, which in turn is connected to our sin. The Hebrew word for holy is *kadosh* which literally means to be separated and set apart. For something to be holy it must be separated from things that would taint it. The Father's holiness depends on being set apart from the unholy sin found in the hearts of humans.

MUCKY PAINT AND SEPARATION

Do you remember painting when you were little? Some cheeky person would always dip their mucky paint-brush in the white paint and make it a funny colour. White paint has to be kept separate from other colours, otherwise it can't keep its whiteness. Holiness is like white paint, it has to be kept away from the things that would compromise its purity. For God to remain holy, he must set some borders and restrictions around himself.

That's why sin is such an issue for God. Adam and Eve knew this and knowing they had something to hide, clothed themselves. I always thought God was being a bit over-cautious about it. I knew that he couldn't come near our sin but I just thought he was being irritable, like one of those people who won't go near someone with a cold. But now I realise it's because he wouldn't be holy otherwise. And that's how we get outside of God's blessing. Our sin places us outside the zone God has set around himself to retain his purity.

It is our sin that separates us from him. The Father is unable to bless us because we are outside his blessing; outside the zone he has set around himself to retain his purity.

David recognised God's purity when he was writing the fifth psalm. David says 'You are not a God who takes pleasure in evil; with you the wicked cannot dwell. The arrogant cannot stand in your presence; you hate all who do wrong' (Ps. 5:4–5).

Why am I telling you about how holy the Father is? To make you think there's no point even trying because we'll never be good enough? To remind us all that we're not clean enough to touch God?

Sometimes, I'm talking to someone and I'm struck by how much cooler or better looking or trendier they are than me. Sometimes, I'm talking to the Father and I'm utterly struck by how much holier and purer and cleaner he is than me. Ever felt the same? Have you ever stood in his presence and realised how far you are from his holiness? There are times when I've stood with my arms wide open in worship and felt so over-whelmed by the Father's presence that I've realised just how impure I am and how completely holy he is, it's almost scary.

His presence is so pure that I beg God to step back because I am so ashamed of how impure I am. Sometimes, the gulf between his holiness and my sin feels like it is so wide we could never really have a rela-tionship. But when we understand just how holy God is and how impure we are, we can begin to understand just how much the Father loves us and how desperately he wants a relationship with us.

LEVITICUS

Leviticus is the central book of the Torah. For the Jews this was more than just the order the books were written, or the fact the middle one looked better there, or it flowed like that, which it doesn't. It was making a statement that Moses' people believed that the book of Leviticus was central to their faith. So even though it breaks up the flow of the narrative of the other four books the Jews placed it there to emphasise its importance to their belief.

To us the book, which is about struggling with sacrifice, offerings and tent maintenance, can be hard work to read. If you have ever given a Bible to a non-Christian friend you can guarantee that they will start from the front and read Genesis and Exodus with ease but then stop when they find themselves in the book of Leviticus.

At the heart of Leviticus is 'Who do we worship?' and 'How do we as a broken people approach the one holy God?' One whom is so holy, that when we stand before him it is so obvious how broken and unholy we are. There are three sacred sections in Leviticus that set out to ensure that the holiness of the people is maintained so that God can be present amongst them. These are: the sacred space called the Tabernacle; the sacred status of God's people, Israel; and thirdly the sacred time found on the *Shabbat* (Sabbath) and special festivals.

The book can be summed up by the verse 'You are to be holy to me because I, YHVH, am holy, and I have set you apart from the nations to be my own' (Lev. 20:26).

God wants his people to be a visual image of what it looks like to be in relationship with the living God, and this image should reflect what God is like in his nature: holy.

God is setting standards that are way higher than those of the people around the Israelites. He takes something that other religions and other people said was fine and told them that it wasn't OK. He was calling them to aspire to his levels of holiness.

Moses is told this directly by God when on Mount Sinai, 'You are to be my holy people. So do not eat the meat of an animal torn by wild beasts; throw it to the dogs' (Ex. 22:31).

GOD HAS STANDARDS AND SO SHOULD WE

The laws in Leviticus were to enable the Jews to meet with the holy God – however, they became orientated to the religion and the Law, and not to God. They forgot that the laws were to enable the worship, not the worship in itself. So Jesus came to show us what it was to be orientated to the Father.

God loves us so much he sent his only Son to die for us, so that we could be set free from the bondage of sin, so that we could have a relationship with the Almighty Holy God of creation. And this realisation moves us towards becoming holier and more like the Father. The Bible makes it clear that we need to be as holy as the Father. God frequently called his people in the Bible to become holy, a nation of people set apart for him and his standards. We shouldn't compare ourselves to other people's levels of holiness because then we'll only ever be able to be as holy as they are. We need to set our sights on God's standards of holiness.

We need to be striving to become more like the Father and not like the Christians around us. That's why being a dancing monkey doesn't work. If we think that worshipping God is a set of rules that we follow then we are like the dancing monkey. We can dance and jig and jump to try and get his blessings but if we're impure our attempts will always be in vain. God doesn't see our pointless dancing, he sees our hearts.

Out of our worship and love of God comes a desire to be closer to him. A realisation that we are broken and God put us back together, that we were lost and he found us. The more time we spend with God, the more time we want to spend with him and the more we want to be like him.

> But he was pierced for our transgressions,
> he was crushed for our iniquities;
> the punishment that brought us peace was upon him,
> and by his wounds we are healed (Is. 53:5).

The word Isaiah used for healed is *hapr* and it can also be translated to mean 'restoration' or 'to come back to perfection' or 'purity'.

Jesus was crucified, died and resurrected and it is because of the wounds he received that we can be made perfect again. The pain he went through and the death he suffered bring us back to purity, back to the way the Father intended it to be, back to a place where we can be like him: holy.

LIVING IT OUT

- Deuteronomy 6:4 talks about God being holy, perfect and whole and says that God doesn't change from day to day. Knowing this, how does it change the way you see your own life, or the way that God wants to respond to you?

- If God is perfectly caring and good, how does this help us respond to the issue of unanswered prayer or suffering?

- The Shema makes it clear that God is one, he is perfect, he is unchanging which means that he is already all-knowing. We can either respond to this by saying 'What's the point in trying to have a relationship with a God who already knows what I am going to say?' or it can inspire us to worship him more. Which response are you inclined to?

- Have you experienced God's perfect love and provision or have you seen this working in someone else's life?

- Why not read through the book of Leviticus particularly the holiness code (which you can find in Lev.

17 – 26)? Try and think through why some of these things might be important to a holy God. Could there be things we need to do today that would help us experience God's holiness more?

FURTHER READING

The Shema: Spirituality and Law in Judaism by Norman Lamm is a Jewish publication but is an extensive commentary on the words of the Shema prayer.

BATHING | 06

SAILORS AND BUBBLE BATH

Do you remember Matey bubble bath? I remember it being a real luxury when I was a child; we hardly ever had it at home because it was too expensive. It sounds silly now but for me, bubble bath in a sailor-shaped bottle was absolute perfection. One day, someone left some at my house. I can't remember who it was or why they brought it but I'm eternally grateful to them. For a while, I looked forward to bath time every night because I knew I'd have that little sailor at my side, but the happiness couldn't last forever and one day, the bottle ran out.

Recently, bath time has become something I look forward to again because I have a little two-year-old boy who loves to spend twenty minutes splashing Daddy and getting the bathroom floor as close to flooded as he can. But bath time isn't fun and games for everyone. For Jews, at the time the Bible was written, bathing wasn't about splashing and bubble bath.

The book of Leviticus in the Old Testament contains what some people call 'the Holiness Code'. It's called this because the words 'holy' and 'holiness' are used repeatedly, which gives us a bit of a clue about the issues God wanted to address. The Code is a collection of laws that are there to teach the Jews, God's people, how to be pure. It is written in one section, 'Anyone . . . who eats anything found dead or torn by wild animals must wash his clothes and bathe with water, and he will be ceremonially unclean till evening; then he will be clean' (Lev. 17:15). In essence it's about bathing in water to keep holy.

The Jewish Holiness Code sounds pretty strict and God constantly asserts his holiness and his authority.

'I, YHVH, am holy.'

'I YHVH, will sanctify.'

These are there to remind God's people of how holy he is and to remind us that we are not holy. The Holiness Code makes it clear that holiness isn't simply about what is in us, our bodies matter to God too. The law states wild things like, if you were unclean by having contact with a woman on her period or because you were suffering from any kind of skin complaint, a ritual purification process had to be taken. These laws are about God wanting his people symbolically pure on the outside, thereby showing what holiness is meant to be like on the inside.

BECOMING A MIRROR

The Holiness Code is God's demand that Israel mirror his holiness. The words 'you shall be holy for I, YHVH your God, am holy', or 'Sanctify yourselves and be holy' appear almost constantly throughout the Old Testament, particularly the Torah.

For the Jewish people, holiness wasn't just about being placed in the Father's blessing. Recognising that the Father is perfect and can't be in the presence of something unclean, the Jewish people made themselves ritually clean before coming to worship the Father.

The Jewish people believed that in order to approach the Father, they needed to perform rites of purification and cleaning which involved full body bathing in huge public areas without the Matey bubble bath. One by one, people would step into huge holes in the ground that were filled with water. The water would be pure spring water that would wash away anything considered ritually unclean. This process would happen as often as needed and could take up to two hours to perform. It would look a bit like adult baptism does today. In fact, John the Baptist had simply taken a common image of purity, one that the

Jewish people would understand, and used it to talk about a new purity that only needed to be done once.

Baptism is our rite of passage and through it we become ritually clean and members of God's family, therefore, we can enter into the holy place of worship.

The holiness laws are rules about . . .

- Worship and how it should be done (Lev. 21:10,21–22)
- Eating naturally dead animals (Lev. 17:15–16)
- Offerings after unlawful sexual involvement (Lev. 19:21–22)
- The Sabbath and Passover (Lev. 23:1–10)
- The cooking of food (Lev. 24:1–9)
- Blasphemy (Lev. 24:10–15,23)
- Property (Lev. 25:23,26–34)
- Slaves (Lev. 25:40,42,44–46)
- Redeeming people (Lev. 25:48–52,54)

WHY DON'T WE KEEP THEM NOW?

The laws are pretty detailed and some seem quite foreign to us but we still need to ask whether God calls us to keep any of these laws today. The laws can be broken into two distinctive groups: religious code as it relates to sin; and lifestyle code as it relates to behaviour.

There are three questions that we can ask to help us decide which of the Holiness Code laws are still applicable.

1. Does Jesus' death on the cross completely fulfil them for us?
2. Were they relevant to the society at the time and therefore no longer an issue in our society?

3. Are the laws ones which still need to be fulfilled by us or are they still relevant?

Many of the religious laws regarding sacrificing animals and birds aren't really applicable today since the Levitical priesthood is no longer possible and ultimately Jesus fulfilled them in his death. Animal sacrifices ended for the Jews with the destruction of the temple where all the sacrifices had to be made. For Christians, the specific sacrifices that occurred daily for individual sin, were replaced by the one-off sacrifice for all our sins by Jesus on the cross. Some laws were of specific relevance to a nomadic tent-dwelling people: they are not relevant in a literal sense now. For example, guidelines about infectious skin diseases (Lev. 13) are to help keep the people healthy, and free from epidemics. Today we would go to a doctor regarding dodgy skin stuff, rather than a priest.

However the holiness laws with regard to behaviour and lifestyle, which include sexuality, are still binding. This is because they are still applicable to today's culture and they're repeated throughout the Bible. Jesus' death allows us forgiveness when we break these laws, if we repent, but he doesn't fulfil them for us. These laws are about trying to help us remain orientated towards God. They also allow us, as God's people to show our inner holiness and forgiveness by behaving in a way that sets us apart from the world on the outside. Some of the laws are also designed by God to keep his people healthy and safe, and as such are still appropriate guidance and advice today. However they are no longer required in order to approach our holy God, as we have already discussed. Since we stand repentant in Jesus we can approach him.

PRIORITIES FOR THE PEOPLE

In the parable of the Good Samaritan, Jesus dealt with whether ritual cleaning is still applicable for us today (Lk. 10:25–37). The story shows how important being ritually pure was to the Jewish leadership but also illustrates how the body can be ritually clean when the heart isn't pure.

One day, a man was attacked by a group of thieves whilst he was walking on the dangerous road between Jerusalem and Jericho. They stole all his belongings, even his clothes and beat him, only leaving when they though he was dead. A priest was walking down the road, on his way to lead worship at the temple. The road would have been no more than two metres wide and so it would have been pretty hard to avoid the dying guy on the road.

In order to understand this section of story we need to make note of one very important thing. For a priest and Levite it was essential that they remained ceremonially clean, otherwise they couldn't do any of their roles at the temple. If they touched a corpse or any human blood they would become ceremonially unclean. It says in Leviticus 22:3 that 'if any of your descendants is ceremonially unclean and yet comes near the sacred offerings that the Israelites consecrate to YHVH, that person must be cut off from my presence.'

For these Jewish leaders the importance of keeping pure for worship outweighed that of helping this dying man or loving their neighbour (also a command in Lev. 19:18).

So to remain ritually clean the priest stepped over the man and went on his way. A little later, a Levite (a special priest's assistant) passed by on his way to the temple. When the Levite saw the man lying in the road, he avoided him and walked as quickly as he could in case he was made unclean by touching him. A short while later a Samaritan came along and took pity on the man. He dressed him and tended to his wounds. The Samaritans were an ethnic group that were the enemies of the Jewish people, yet the man showed the Jewish traveller pity, respect and even love.

What was Jesus trying to teach us here? He was teaching us about serving others, even when it's out of our way and he was teaching us to love our neighbour, whoever they may be. But Jesus was also commenting on ritual cleansing.

The priest and the Levite were aware that if they touched the dying man in the road they would be made ritually unclean. They wouldn't have been able to participate in the worship at the Temple, which was the reason they were travelling on the road in the first place.

Jesus was implying this question: Is it more pleasing to God that we remain ritually clean or that we help someone desperately in need of help, even if it means getting dirty?

In Mark's Gospel, a Jewish teacher of the Law came to Jesus with criticism about how Jesus and his followers followed the Holiness Code. The teachers, seeing that Jesus and his followers ate without ritually cleaning their hands, began to question the example Jesus was setting.

Jesus responded to the teachers of the Law pretty strongly: 'Thus you nullify [cancel out] the word of God by your tradition that you have handed down. And you do many things like that' (Mk. 7:13). Then Jesus spoke about the issue of purity to the crowd that gathered around him: '"Listen to me, everyone . . . Nothing outside a man can make him 'unclean' by going into him. Rather, it is what comes out of a man that makes him 'unclean'."'

Later, when Jesus was hanging out with the disciples he brought it up again

> "Don't you see that nothing that enters a man from the outside can make him 'unclean'? For it doesn't go into his heart but into his stomach, and then out of his body . . . What comes out of a man is what makes him 'unclean'. For from within, out of men's hearts, come evil thoughts, sexual immorality, theft, murder, adultery, greed, malice, deceit, lewdness, envy, slander, arrogance and folly. All these evils come from inside and make a man 'unclean'" (18–23).

HOLY ON THE INSIDE

I recently had a long chat over coffee with my friend, the rabbi, about Jewish ideas of purity. Judah emphasised the importance of ideas about cleansing and purity in the Jewish faith today. He also highlighted how prominent these ideas are in the Bible. The first clash Jesus had with the Pharisees was about the Jewish laws on purity and the debate continued throughout most of the New Testament.

It's interesting that the Pharisees didn't ask Jesus about his views on creation or prayer or sermon methods. It is clear from the questions they asked that the centre of their faith was holiness and purity. The teachers of the Law aren't interested in the theological stance of Jesus or his views on what was happening at the time, they want to know what he thought about the Jewish rituals of purity.

Jesus brought a new perspective to the Holiness Code. Jesus broke the link between being holy on the inside and being clean on the outside. You can be covered in dirt but have a pure heart and you can be beautifully clean on the outside and have a heart turned away from God. It's about what's going on in our hearts. Jesus taught that holiness is about being placed in the Father's blessing and then allowing that to change our hearts and minds.

But at the same time Paul writes to the Thessalonians that it is the Father's will that we should be sanctified. The original Greek word for 'sanctified' is linked to the words holy and ritually clean. In other words, it is the Father's will that we should be ritually clean. But it's more than that. Paul writes in 1 Thessalonians 4:7 that not only does God want us to be holy but he requires us to daily live a holy life.

There's a new way to holiness; we are made clean and set free from these laws because we have received the Father's blessing through Jesus. But, we're still asked to be holy people.

The Father has called us to be holy.

What does it mean to be called to this? A calling is when we have been divinely asked to do something specific for God. But what does the holiness we are called to look like?

Paul clearly unpacks what holiness is in very practical terms.

> It is God's will that you should be sanctified: that you should avoid sexual immorality; that each of you should learn to control his own body in a way that is holy and honourable, not in passionate lust like the heathen, who do not know God; and that in this matter no one should wrong his brother or take advantage of him. The Lord will punish men for all such sins, as we have already told you and warned you. For God did not call us to be impure, but to live a holy life (1 Thes. 4:3–7).

HOLY IN THE SACK

Whenever I teach on purity or holiness, the first thing people bring up is sex. I don't think it's just the mind of teenagers either; people often link sex with impurity. The evangelical church often makes sex into a big deal, the focus of so much teaching and time that I don't think is always that helpful. But, in his practical guide to holiness, Paul addresses sexual sin first, so we will too.

Many young Christians have been pretty messed up and confused by what they've been taught about sex by church leaders and family members, thinking that sex is a bad thing, something to keep away from because it's unholy and impure, something that Satan uses to get to people.

Other churches avoid any teaching on it, afraid of alienating their congregation and young people if they challenge in any way the world's view on sex.

Both teachings screw up the way we see one of the Father's holy gifts. The Bible teaches us that God wants us to enjoy sex and see it as a gift, within certain guidelines. We know that all of God's gifts are holy, so sex is holy – imagine that.

The thing at stake here is keeping orientated towards God. Uncontrolled sexual desire leads us to sin and moves us away from the Father. God wants us to master our desires in a holy and honourable way so that we don't place the god of sex before him; that we don't direct ourselves away from God at the centre of our lives and towards other things. Purity is orientating ourselves towards God.

So many people think they're not holy or pure anymore because they've had sex and I want to reassure you that you can still be pure even if you're not a virgin. It's all about re-orientating yourself to Jesus: you will never be a virgin again but you will be holy.

Sometimes, it feels like the words 'sex' and 'holiness' don't go together at all, but that's not the work of God. Satan constantly tries to create an atmosphere of impurity around sex so we won't see the beauty and the holiness of one of God's gifts.

Sex is holy, something that is special and made for a committed relationship.

'Love is patient, love is kind. It does not envy, it does not boast, it is not proud. It is not rude, it is not self-seeking, it is not easily angered and it keeps no record of wrongs' (1 Cor. 13:4–5). Now, I'll admit that this passage might seem a little cheesy, like something you'd find in a greetings card but it's really important. The biblical view of sex is so tied up with love that if we're thinking about sex we need to think about this passage. Real love isn't self-seeking; it doesn't use someone else to get sexual gratification. Sex within marriage is meant to be an image of the intimacy we have with God.

SEX AND THE SHEMA

Recently my rabbi friend Judah told me that the Jewish understanding of sexual purity is about knowing the Shema. It seems like the Shema has the answer to a lot of life's questions. 'Love YHVH your God with all your heart and with all your soul and with all your strength' (Deut. 6:4). Later Jesus decreed this the most important commandment and also tied it to 'love your neighbour as yourself' (Mk. 12:31).

If we start to get to grips with the 'oneness' of God's love and the total purity and holiness of that love, we can begin to see the model of a godly relationship and how we then respond by loving God and loving our neighbour.

So many of our relationships are based on self-interest and self-gratification, getting what we want and need. But a pure love is not just about trying to please someone else: it's a lot deeper than that. The Shema holds within its words the idea that true love comes only from the Father and that this love awakens a much deeper understanding of loving our neighbour.

Judah said that 'As we gaze upon the gorgeousness and oneness of God [and I'd add the gorgeousness of the Cross] we slowly realise how shallow our understanding of love truly is. God daily shows me the extent to which my so-called love is still fairly shallow.'

So many of our ideas about sex somehow miss the point, we sell it short. We need to understand the God-givenness of physical sexual feelings and to discover that love and sex go deeply together.

We are called to be ritually pure in our sex life: we need to learn to love our partners sexually and not understanding this as physically but with our hearts and our whole beings. That is why waiting for the right person and for marriage is so important.

Sex is holy!

HOLY AT NIGHT

After dealing with sexual self-control, Paul widens his argument to unpack ideas about self-control in general.

> You are all sons and daughters of the light and sons and daughters of the day. We do not belong to the night or to the darkness. So then, let us not be like others, who are asleep, but let us be alert and self-controlled. For those who sleep, sleep at night, and those who get drunk, get drunk at night. But since we belong to the day, let us be

> self-controlled, putting on faith and love as a breastplate
> and the hope of salvation as a helmet (1 Thes. 5:5–8).

We can tell from this passage that, even thousands of years ago, all the dodgy stuff went on at night. There is something powerful and drawing about the night. We tend to drink more at night, we think more about things we shouldn't and we do and say things we often wouldn't in the day. Paul noticed that there's something about the night, maybe it's because we feel like our actions are hidden and things are easier to get away with. For instance, most people don't look at pornography during the day; it must feel much more secret and private to use it at night.

We are called to separate ourselves from things that are done at night, drunkenness, sexual deviance and shameful lusts.

Have you ever noticed that moths fly straight to the light when it's dark outside, clustering around light bulbs and candles? As God's holy people, that's how we are called to be, clinging to the light because Satan is looking out for times when we are at our most secretive and vulnerable.

> Be self-controlled and alert. Your enemy the devil prowls around like a roaring lion looking for someone to devour. Resist him, standing firm in the faith, because you know that your brothers throughout the world are undergoing the same kind of sufferings (1 Pet. 5:8–9).

Paul is also calling us to have control over anything that will draw us away from the Father's blessing, from things that have control over us and push God out of the centre of our lives.

In the book of Romans Paul make a comprehensive list of such things.

Sexual impurity, worshipping and serving created things rather than the Creator, indulging shameful lusts, exchanging natural relations for unnatural ones, committing indecent acts with other men and women, wickedness, evilness, greed, depravity, envy, murder, strife, being deceitful and malicious, gossiping, slandering, God-hating, being insolent, being arrogant, being boastful, disobeying our parents, being senseless, being faithless, being heartless and being ruthless.

Paul also says that mankind creates new ways of doing evil all the time and then approves of those who practice them. So we need to be careful not to look at the list and say 'I don't do any of those' because we could be practicing a more modern sin or even creating a brand new one (Rom 1:21–33).

Satan wants to destroy us, which is why he prowls around like a roaring lion, looking for victims to devour. It's important to recognise that at night we are often drawn to things we shouldn't be and that's when Satan steps in and gets in between God and us. Satan is powerful but not God's equal; God has already defeated him. He is only given some freedom for a period of time and his time is coming to an end. We can't necessarily understand why God allows Satan this freedom but we can be certain that God is, and will always be, in control.

HOLY IN ACTION

So, being full of self-control keeps us close to God and away from sin. Paul writes in all his letters about having self-control in what we eat, the words we speak, the way we express anger and the way we boast. Lack of self-control is the underpinning of all sin as we allow our feelings to overtake our thoughts. Even the Ten Commandments all boil down to the need to be controlled in our actions and our choices. For instance, somebody who commits murder has let their anger get completely out of control.

Peter writes that we need to make sure our thoughts are clear, that we are able to control all of our actions. We need to love each other more, being hospitable and selfless without grumbling. Peter calls all believers to be generous with the gifts the Father has given us, serving others faithfully and administering God's living grace in all forms (1 Pet. 4).

WHAT DOES THIS LOOK LIKE ON THE GROUND?

We have begun to build up a picture of how holiness looks in our lives. We see that when we seek a holy lifestyle, one characterised by self-control, we stay close to God and in the light. Sex is no longer something of which to be ashamed, it's something to be respected and seen as holy. When we are full of self-control our words, our actions, our thoughts and the way we treat people all reflect God and they're full of light.

We can see that holiness isn't just an idea or something to aim towards: it's a lifestyle that is possible for us. In fact, it's more than possible, it's our calling. God clearly commands us to stop sinning and be holy as God is holy. Sometimes, it seems impossible to ever stop living in the dark. The habits we have, and the things we're used to, make it hard to live a holy life. But, we have the Almighty God there to help us and if God's called us to do something God will always help us to do it. God promises us everything we need for life, purity and godliness.

But how holy can we be?

Peter writes 'But just as he who called you is holy, so be holy in all you do; for it is written: "Be holy, because I am holy"' (1 Pet. 1:15–16).

Holiness is the very character and being of the Father and he wants us, his sons and daughters, to act and be like him.

Peter also tells us that we are 'a chosen people, a royal priesthood, a holy nation' (1 Pet. 2:9). Paul then pushes this idea of a holy church one step further by writing in the book of Ephesians, 'and to present her (the church) to himself as a radiant church, without stain or wrinkle or any other blemish, but holy and blameless' (Eph. 5:27).

Have you ever looked at the people around you at church? Do you see them as holy, as radiant and blameless? I find it hard too. We're just a bunch of people working out what it means to love God and reflect that in our lives.

But God says he sees his people as holy.

The writer of the book of Hebrews understood the importance of us being set apart and holy. He says 'make every effort to live in peace with all people and to be holy; without holiness no one will see the Lord' (12:14).

The key to holiness is thirsting and desperately wanting to be holy. If we think it is impossible then we are already presuming that we can't grow in holiness. We need to thirst for holiness to change us inwardly and outwardly.

A few years ago we had one of the hottest summers in Britain, with temperatures reaching over 33 degrees centigrade. Never have I understood more of what it means to thirst for God. Every Tuesday as a church we go to our local park for football. Guys and girls from church and our community turn up for a kick around. On one of the hottest weeks of that summer I stupidly forgot to bring a bottle of water. We played for ninety minutes and by the end of the match I'd collapsed on the floor, almost fainting with thirst and the heat. I was boiling, my mouth was dry and I had nothing to drink. I was absolutely desperate for water.

We need to be that thirsty for a lifestyle of holiness. We're pretty much stuffed without it. For without holiness, without clothing ourselves in Jesus, without orientating ourselves away from the stuff that gets in the way, we will never see the Father.

IT'S ALL ABOUT HIS PRIORITIES

Sadly, many of us have chosen a lifestyle based on our priorities not God's. To change we have to realise that we need to get rid of our own ideas of relationships, money and popularity and decide to deepen our relationship with Jesus. When our spirit is reborn, our lifestyle follows.

Paul wrote to the Philippians, saying

> But whatever was to my profit I now consider loss for the sake of Christ. What is more, I consider everything a loss compared to the surpassing greatness of knowing Christ Jesus my Lord, for whose sake I have lost all things. I consider them rubbish, that I may gain Christ (3:7–8).

To gain Christ means to have a real relationship with him, giving up parts of your lifestyle and changing the way you are. It's about swapping the things you used to value for something else, holiness.

But we don't have to change stuff by ourselves. We need to let the Father pour out his spirit on us, filling us with a thirst for holiness and desperation to be changed. John made the connection between God's presence and our recognition that we aren't living right. 'When he comes, he will convict the world of guilt in regard to sin and righteousness and judgment' (Jn. 16:8).

We probably all know someone who has come to faith but found it hard to square up their lifestyle with their new beliefs. We often try to carry on living as we were before we knew God, which ends up getting confusing. As we pointed out earlier, the way we live can distract us from our walk with the Father and we start to fall back into old routines. We wander away from the place of blessing and feel more and more distant from God.

VITAL TO OUR FAITH

Living a holy life is vital to our walk with the Father. A jigsaw can never be finished until all the pieces are put together. The jigsaw of faith is made up of several pieces and if one is missing it makes it hard to see the picture it's meant to reveal, the image of us walking with our maker.

If we don't have all the pieces of prayer, worship, Bible study, self-control, holiness, seeking justice for the poor, walking humbly and seeking God's constant revelation, our faith is weaker and we get more and more distant from God.

This is still all about making sure we orientate ourselves to Christ; other things do not seem to matter any more when we do this. We are no longer worthless, we see over and over again that we are valuable and precious, but at the same time, we are not worthy of the life given to us. When we come to the realisation that this life is not ours but that we have been bought by Jesus on the cross, then we can actually say that this life is for Christ and we need to live it in such a way he sees as fitting.

So, through baptism we are ritually pure and able to enter into the eternal act of worship. And we are called to live a life of love and self-control, keeping us close to the Father and in his special place of blessing.

As we clothe ourselves in Jesus we stand before God a holy people. But at the same time a thirst and desire for holiness challenges us to sort out whatever has the potential to get in the way of orientating ourselves to God. It is not about being the dancing monkey to gain the Father's love, but it is about dancing in pleasure and joy with a life of love and self-control because we know that the Father loves us, and delights in our holy actions.

LIVING IT OUT

- Israel was called to mirror God's holiness to a broken world. How do you think the worldwide church fails to mirror this holy God to the world?

- How do you think the church in general mirrors God well? We tend to be able to see the negatives more than the positives. Try spending more time on this question than the previous one or writing a longer 'positives' list than 'negatives'.

- If it is correct that God sees his people as holy, how does this help us to respond to a world that is so unholy? Do we become a holy ghetto, or do we try to reveal Jesus to those around us? And if you think the answer's the second one – how do we actually put this into practice?

- Sadly, many of us have chosen a lifestyle this is more about our priorities than God's priorities. How do we find out God's priorities and make them a reality in our lives?

- If holiness isn't just an ideal but our calling, how do you think this should change our response to the issue? Are there things you need to be aiming towards in trying to live out holiness on the ground? For example, for me it might be about changing the way I consume the world's resources or the way that I respond to unhelpful thoughts.

FURTHER READING

The Politics of Jesus by John Howard Yoder is a practical and insightful book discussing what holiness means on a political level.

God's Politics by Jim Wallis is also helpful, looking at holiness played out in a political world.

The Holiness of God by R.C. Sproul examines how we need to be better reflectors of God's holiness and how this should look on the ground.

MITZVAH | 07

MICHAEL JACKSON AND NOAH

Who was your childhood inspiration?

We all have people we look up to. I don't think I have one person in particular, just lots of people that I admire for lots of different reasons.

A while ago I was at a Christian conference and the speaker got us to call out the names of our childhood heroes. The list was fantastic ranging from the normal to the weird to the extremely weird. There were people whose heroes were weatherwomen, writers, theologians, scientists and long distance drivers. One guy wanted to be Batman because when he was little he liked to hide in dark places. Interesting . . .

But my personal favourite was a guy who revealed that he'd wanted to be like Noah. As in Noah and the Ark. The guy's two childhood passions were building things and playing with animals so he recognised that Noah was the perfect hero for him as he combined both of these qualities. He said that he'd actually prayed to be a modern day Noah, someone called by God to build a massive floating zoo. I think he overlooked the fact that the first big flood wiped out the whole of mankind except for Noah and his family, something I'm sure the guy didn't want to happen. The guy's story reminded me of a joke, which I shared.

Q. What type of lights would Noah have had on the ark?

A. Flood lights

Everyone giggled a bit (I think they were still in shock over the whole Noah hero thing) and then I shared who my hero was. I told the group I had wanted to be like Michael Jackson. It was a fairly short phase but I spent quite a bit of time practicing dance moves in front of the TV. One year, whilst on holiday with my parents, I put on a bright red tracksuit and a white glove and performed in a talent contest to 'Thriller'. But I never really wanted to be him; I just wanted to be able to dance like him.

I've always found that I look up to those around me rather than people from television or films or the radio. I started to learn guitar because someone at school played. It wasn't that I wanted to be like him, I just wanted to play guitar like him. When I was studying at Art College I was surrounded by loads of really talented artists who really inspired me to be more creative and to try new things. Even now, the example they set still pushes me to use my creativity in all that I do.

I love seeing what others are doing creatively so that I can take ideas and develop them for my church.

Creative people inspire me to be more creative. Deep thinkers inspire me to think more deeply.

PEOPLE FORM US

We don't always realise it but the people around us help to form who we are. We see things we like in other people and try to be more like that.

Who inspires you?

Who do you want to be like?

Who was your childhood hero?

Can you see how they helped to form who you are? Can you see the things that you've picked up from the people around you? Let's hope that they're a good influence.

When we meet people who are better at something than we are, it can humble us to want to grow and become more like them.

If we find ourselves before the Father, looking into his 'oneness', his almighty glory and omnipotence, we soon find ourselves becoming humble. We recognise that we need to become more like him but acknowledge we can never fully become like him.

God is pleased when we're in this place of humility, when we're in his blessing and overwhelmed that we're not like him. It's how it should be and God gives grace to us when we're in this place.

Peter understood this when he wrote, 'Humble yourselves, therefore, under God's mighty hand, that he may lift you up in due time' (1 Pet. 5:6).

Peter recognised that there is a process. We start off caught up in our sin and full of pride but as we stand in the Father's blessing, we find ourselves becoming more and more humble. As we spend time with the Father, we are both brought low and lifted up. We bow down because we realise that God is holy, and we are sinful, but then God raises us up by giving us grace. Humility brings greatness but a different kind of greatness.

William Temple once said that 'Humility does not mean thinking less of yourself than of other people, nor does it mean having a low opinion of your own gifts. It means freedom from thinking about yourself at all.'[14]

Humility is about freedom from ourselves and our own minds.

DEEP FAITH IN THE DIVINE

Our humbleness should spring from a deep faith and a fear of the Almighty God. As we think about the miracle of creation, knowing that the Father is the creator of all things seen and unseen, as we see billions of people created by God, each person intricately different but perfectly created, we should realise just how small and insignificant we actually are. We could die at any second, we are weak and we grow old.

Compared to the omnipotent, eternal, omniscient Creator, we are tiny and vulnerable. We are weak and so sinful, yet God loves us wholeheartedly and completely.

We are loved by a divine, all-knowing, all-powerful God.

We should be humble because God's holiness brings us to our knees. The Bible is full of stories about God using humble people like Moses, Samuel and David. God could only use Jesus in a massive plan to save mankind because Jesus was so humble. Even though he was God, he put aside his majesty to come down to earth.

On the night before he died Jesus 'fell with his face to the ground and prayed, "My Father, if it is possible, may this cup be taken from me. Yet not as I will, but as you will"' (Mt. 26:39). Jesus humbled himself for the use of the Father, '*not my will, but yours*'. The Father recognised his son's humbleness and chose after his death and resurrection to exalt him, so now he is seated at the right hand of the Father where he is worshipped and glorified. Jesus is our greatest example of humility.

LITTLE GODS AND THE BIG GOD

A poet called Oliver Holmes once said a very profound thing about humility. 'Most of us retain enough of the theological attitude to think that we are little gods."[15] How do you see your identity? Do you have an inflated view of yourself? Often our self-esteem is linked to what's happening in our lives at the time. If you were to be in the next indie band, when do you think you would be the most humble? While playing Wembley stadium or when you were playing a small venue down a back alley? We need to be careful that our view of ourselves comes from the Father and not the world, nor even Wembley stadium.

So, as we come closer to the Father, we become aware that God is greater than us and we are humbled, knowing that we can never be as holy as he is. We need to humble ourselves every day, reminding ourselves that God is perfect and we are not.

TO FORGIVE LIKE GOD

Humility and forgiveness have to go hand in hand. How can you be forgiving and not be humble? Let me explain. If you are to forgive someone who has done something against you, which left you really hurt, you are making yourself their servant. To not forgive can be a position of power, implying you think yourself more important than them. To be humble means to take no advantage of the situation but to give them the advantage of your freedom.

As Christians, we need to be aware of how sinful we are and how God forgives us, even though we don't deserve it. When we don't forgive others, we aren't mirroring God's holy example.

Forgiveness is when the rubber hits the road. Forgiveness is one of the hardest parts of God's holiness to live out in our own lives. Being unwilling to forgive is not an attribute of holiness, neither is it something from God. We forgive because we have been forgiven. We need to remember that our holiness and purity depends on the biblical teaching on forgiveness: if we are unable to forgive then we cannot be holy. Let me explain.

One day Jesus was approached by his twelve followers who asked him to teach them how to pray. They weren't merely asking Jesus how to pray or how prayer works, since they were Jews and would have been taught how to pray from a young age. They wanted to know how to pray with power and authority like Jesus did. The disciples knew that Jesus had a special relationship with the Father and wanted in on it.

> One day Jesus was praying in a certain place. When he finished, one of his disciples said to him, "Lord, teach us to pray, just as John taught his disciples."
> He said to them, "When you pray, say:
> 'Father,
> hallowed be your name,
> your kingdom come.
> Give us each day our daily bread.
> Forgive us our sins,
> for we also forgive everyone who sin against us . . .'"
> (Lk. 11:1–4).

Forgive our sins as we forgive those who sin against us.

Do you really want God to forgive us in the same way we forgive? So often we forgive half-heartedly, saying one thing with our mouths but holding on to grudges in our hearts: that's not forgiveness. God's forgiveness never remembers our sin; he puts it right out of his mind. When we ask to receive God's total forgiveness we have to be willing to give others the same forgiveness.

God's forgiveness should humble us and make us want to forgive like he does. We should forgive others as a response to God's love not as an attempt to earn God's love and forgiveness.

How can we be forgiven if we are unwilling to forgive others? If we are clinging to the past we must also be clinging to the ways of our past that aren't of God. When we ask for God's forgiveness we are essentially asking that things are made right with him. How can we ask this when we aren't really at peace with someone else? Being truly sorry is turning away from old things and starting again.

If we're not at peace with others, can we really be at peace with the Father? Isn't it devaluing the grace given to you by God if you don't value that grace in your relationships with other people?

613 COMMANDMENTS AND REBUILDING WORK

My friend Judah and I were debating the Jewish understanding of forgiveness. He was telling me about how his son had broken the command to honour your mother and father by telling a lie. To put things right, his son had to recognise his sin, confess it to his parents and do '*mitzvah*'.

Mitzvah is a word used within Judaism to refer to the 613 commandments found in the Torah. The term *mitzvah* in modern Judaism has also come to express any act that makes amends for your sin. Essentially the world is broken because of our sin and God is looking for people to help him put it back together again.

Judah understands *mitzvah* as a three-fold response to our sin. Firstly, we need to admit the sin and name it, secondly we need to confess the sin to the person we have sinned against and finally, we need to try and make things right. For example, if I broke something, to make things right I might repair or replace it. If I said something bad about someone I might need to publicly commit an act of kindness so others saw me putting things right with the person.

This is not seen as a traditional Christian response to sin or forgiveness. Most Christians would agree with admitting the sin to God, but the rest isn't seen as a necessary part of the Christian idea of God's forgiveness. We understand that our forgiveness doesn't rest on any act of amendment or doing *mitzvah*, although it might be an honourable thing to do in many cases.

God requires us to acknowledge our sin and confess it. But could this be our way of keeping confession and our response at arms length almost like a cheap 'Sorry'? What if God's response to our sin requires us to help in the rebuilding of a broken world that we have helped to break. Judah shared an old Jewish story with me, which really helped me to understand the Jewish concept of *mitzvah*. It would have been a story Jesus would have known, even if in a slightly different form.

> One day two Jewish men were travelling down the same road. One of the men was rich, the other was rather poor. During the journey one of the two men turned to the other, taking a dislike to the other man, started to verbally abuse him, telling him he looked cheap and poor.
>
> Both men arrived at the same destination. When the rich man realised they had both come to the same place he was saddened to find out that the poor man he had abused on the journey was, in fact, a guest rabbi at the synagogue.
>
> After he had taken the service the rich man came to the poor rabbi and begged for him to forgive him. The rabbi refused to do this telling him that he needed to go to the real man he had insulted. 'Go and apologise to the real poor men and women you offended on the road.'

Judah explained that the Jewish understanding of the story was that the person was only genuine in his repentance and apology when he was prepared to go and do something about it. On the other hand, the forgiveness was only given when the person wronged against was willing to grant it. In the Jewish faith, forgiveness is not in the hands of the one doing the confessing, it's in the hands of the one who was wronged. If I refuse to forgive someone, they remain unforgiven, both by me and by God.

GOD'S RESPONSE TO A BROKEN WORLD

Mitzvah makes it clear that true repentance still cannot be earned, but simply by helping to put back together the lives we have hurt we enter into God's response to our injustice. In this we also acknowledge to God that we have hurt people, showing we see all sides of the act. Jesus taught that if we are truly sorry and confess our sins to the Father we will be forgiven, even when we haven't received freedom from others. This could seem to be a contradiction, but it is simply about God helping us to be set free from the burden of not forgiving.

We find a perfect example of *mitzvah* in the New Testament. In Matthew chapter 26 Jesus is taken away and Peter was sitting in the courtyard, when three times he was asked if he knew Jesus. Each time he said no, until the third time when he said no, and then called curses down on himself (vv. 69–75).

'If I know him may I die right here' or 'May God punish me if I am lying.'[16]

At this point the crow crowed and Peter went outside and wept bitterly, or a better translation might be, 'cried like a baby'. Peter realised what he had done and was devastated. He went back to fishing because he thought he had totally stuffed up; he had allowed the world to continue to be broken by adding to the lies in the world. Jesus is led to his death, and placed in the tomb, three days later the tomb is empty and there is resurrection in the air. Jesus joins the fishermen for breakfast on the beach (Jn. 21).

Jesus sits with Peter and starts to put Peter back together again. Three times Jesus asks Peter if he loves him. Why three times? Could it be that Jesus is doing *mitzvah*? That Jesus is helping rebuild Peter by counteracting the three times he had said he didn't know Jesus. Jesus ends with 'feed my sheep' (v. 17) which is essentially a euphemism for 'look after my people, make sure they get what they need'. It is as though Jesus is saying you're done, you have been reinstated, your lies, which have cracked you, have been put back together.

This *mitzvah* is the resurrection of Jesus at work. The resurrection does three things. Firstly it saves us from something, which can be sin, or the suffering from sin. Secondly it is about being saved for something like the afterlife, heaven or a greater task. And thirdly it's about being saved through a process of healing and transformation, from brokenness to wholeness or God's 'one-ness'.

In what ways are we like Peter and deny Jesus therefore needing forgiveness and mending through the resurrection. Sometimes the subtle ways we do it are the worst. What about the times when we talk about others, or we make choices in lifestyle issues that simply say 'I don't live Jesus' way.'

We don't need to say we don't follow Jesus for people to hear those words. Often our actions speak much louder and every time we do something Scripture forbids we tell the world that we don't respect Jesus. For example, if we buy things that have been made by people in dreadful conditions, or copy CDs and DVDs or choose cars that are not fuel-efficient and thus pump out even more fumes than other models, hastening environmental destruction.

When we don't forgive, surely this too tells the world that we don't know Jesus? God forgives us when we don't deserve it, but if we remain unforgiving against others we sin against God. Forgiveness has to be given freely and not earned. But we still make people try to earn forgiveness, don't we? Have you ever made someone work for your forgiveness?

We know that working or payment for forgiveness is not consistent with what the Bible teaches. But Jesus would have grown up with this understanding of forgiveness and on a few occasions, he referred to it. Jesus taught that the Father forgives for reasons of his own, not because we purchased it with actions. But John indicates this Jewish view of the final step of forgiveness being in the hands of the wronged party.

> Again Jesus said, 'Peace be with you! As the Father has sent me, I am sending you.' And with that he breathed on them and said, 'Receive the Holy Spirit. If you forgive anyone his sins, they are forgiven; if you do not forgive them, they are not forgiven (Jn. 20:21–24).

WE HAVE RESPONSIBILITY TO SET THEM FREE

What if we realised that us forgiving someone released them from the sin just as if we handed over something physical to show how we gave them forgiveness. This concept shows a wonderful understanding that the one wronged has the power to absolve the sin. We have a decision whether to allow them to be sin-free; by absolution they are then set free from the power of the sin.

The Bible specifically directs us to offer our forgiveness freely, without holding a grudge. It seems that when we refuse to forgive someone, it has a negative impact on us: 'Do not judge and you will not be judged. Do not condemn, and you will not be condemned. Forgive, and you will be forgiven' (Lk. 6:37).

'And when you stand praying, if you hold anything against anyone, forgive him, so that your Father in heaven may forgive you your sins' (Mk. 11:25).

These are directions rather than suggestions yet they make no reference to the needs of the person who has wronged us. It's clear that choosing to forgive is the best option. We need to let God free us and heal us, so we can grow closer to him and become more like him. If we don't forgive, we can never be released from the anger and the pain of being wronged. Only through releasing forgiveness can we receive the healing needed.

The reason God has given us this specific command is because he does not want anything to stand between him and us. God's love for us is beyond our comprehension. Forgiving others spares us from the consequences of living out life with an unforgiving heart.

Forgiving someone isn't dependent on how they've wronged us. Just as God sees all sin as equal, all needing repentance and forgiveness, we need to forgive all sin equally. God didn't list certain sins as unforgivable or say that forgiveness was optional for some sins. Some sins hurt us more than others and have bigger consequences but they still need to be forgiven like all other sins. Our Father makes it clear that we need to forgive everyone, each time they hurt us, without fail.

We all have stories about times when we have needed to forgive someone. Some of these stories are really painful and hard for us to talk about, whilst some make us smile.

IT'S YOURS

At a church I worked at a few years ago, we decided to run a Christian skate park as part of a weeklong outreach programme. The Christian part didn't change the way we skated nor did we ever put the ramps in the shape of a cross but the park did run with Christian rules of grace, mercy, love and forgiveness. It was an amazing time and we saw lots of young people coming to faith whilst skating on our half pipe.

Right at the beginning, one of the skaters had his skateboard stolen. It was taken while he was grabbing a drink from the café; it just vanished. Phil was gutted; he'd saved for ages to get a new deck and he'd only had it a short while.

Phil used a battered old skateboard for the rest of the skating events and on the last day a skateboard caught his eye. It belonged to one of the younger guys and it looked suspiciously like the skateboard that had been stolen. Remembering that he'd done some graffiti art on the underside of the deck, Phil asked the younger guy if he could see the board. Defensively, the guy handed over the deck. It was obvious that the deck was Phil's, and seeing him take a step towards the guy, a couple of people came inside to get me, fearing that there would be a fight. I ran outside and was totally amazed to see that Phil had handed his precious skateboard back to the young guy, telling him that he was giving it to him so that he was no longer a thief.

By handing the deck over to the young guy Phil was forgiving him and setting him free from his sin.

Could you do the same?

Could you hand your iPod to a thief telling him he could have it, therefore he hadn't stolen it? Could you give your bike or wallet to a burglar saying he could have it, therefore forgiving him for his action?

It sounds a crazy idea but I saw it happen and it was amazing, it was beautiful. That image of Phil and the skater guy will never leave my mind. That is what forgiveness is, that is what freedom is.

IT'S FOR THE PRESENT

Please remember that forgiving someone does not just-ify their action or their crime. Neither does it provide them with eternal forgiveness, only God can do that. Nothing can ever undo their past or our past, but we can do something about our present and future condition. Remember, forgiveness and grace from us makes a way for their and our healing to begin. This forgiveness and reconciliation often starts as a decision of surrendering our hurt and pain. This surrender invites God to begin working in our lives in a much deeper level, allowing God to heal us.

It needs to be noted that some of us are victims of unspeakable painful things and the thought of ever looking the person in the eye or even speaking to them again is just too far away from where you are. Although God does ask for us to forgive, as it sets us free as well as them, he will give us time, space and strength to do that.

I have heard of people who have taken years to get to a point of even talking about an event that broke them. Years had passed and slowly they were able to speak about how they had been damaged. And day by day, through the power of Jesus' resurrection they were able to get to a point of saying 'I could never understand why they did this to me but I will forgive them, they are free of this.'

An attitude of holiness is one of being open to making the choice of forgiveness and reconciliation. It's one of the hardest attributes of God's holiness but we have a divine example for forgiving others in Christ.

The Father knew that we needed to see a real physical symbol of forgiveness to show it was possible, which is why he sent us his son Jesus, the son whom we can now clothe ourselves in.

This is how God showed his love among us: He sent his one and only Son into the world that we might live through him. This is love: not that we loved God, but that he loved us and sent his Son as an atoning sacrifice for our sins (1 Jn. 4:9–10).

Writing to the Colossians about Christ's example of forgiveness, Paul said, 'Bear with each other and forgive whatever grievances you may have against one another. Forgive as the Lord forgave you' (Col. 3:13).

The son of the Father not only had the authority to forgive us but also the authority to grant us the ability to do the same.

If this chapter has challenged you but you're still unsure about how to forgive someone, you could say the prayer written below. Think about what the words you are saying mean, and let God speak to you and bring you healing.

Almighty Father,
Thank you for the forgiveness I have seen through your son Jesus on the cross. Lord, I ask that you would help me gain a better understanding of how I can forgive freely those who have hurt me and the people I care about. Would you help heal broken relationships and bring forgiveness, more deeply than I can even understand? Show me your true pure humility and grace so that I can be humbled by your glory, therefore making me more humble and generous. Help me to freely forgive and thank you that you have freely forgiven me. I pray all of this in Jesus' holy name, by whom all forgiveness and healing was made possible. Thank you for loving me in ways I'll never comprehend.
In Jesus' name,
Amen.

LIVING IT OUT

- What Christians around you do you admire? What is it about them that makes you respect them?

- Is humility a trait that you see in them? How does this inspire you to become more humble?

- How do you see humility and forgiveness going together? Without humility do you think it's easy to be forgiving?

- How have others who have forgiven you set you free?

- Where have you seen true forgiveness played out in your own life? Has there been an incident or a time where you saw someone forgive someone else and been inspired by it?

- How do you think forgiveness is revolutionary to the world around you? Do you think it's countercultural?

- In what areas do you need to become more humble so that you might be more forgiving?

FURTHER READING

Living in the Grace of God by Rob Rufus is a powerful book looking at living in the place of forgiveness and how this enables us to grow and flourish in becoming more like Jesus.

RIGHTEOUSNESS | 08

GOOD BOOKS AND THE GOOD BOOK

The Da Vinci Code and other similar books have inspired me to study the Bible harder than I ever have before, getting to grips with what it says, its history and how it was put together. I love reading about how the Bible was collated and how people prayerfully brought the individual books. Now, don't get me wrong, *The Da Vinci Code* said some shocking things about the Bible and about the life of Jesus but it did make me want to check out what it said. Some people would say that what Dan Brown wrote can basically be termed a 'load of old crock' but at least it got me passionate about seeking the truth of Scripture again.

There's a real longing in our culture for knowledge, isn't there? There are thousands of articles every day about the intimate details of celebrities, so it feels like we know them, even though we've never met them. There are thousands of guidebooks so you can know everything about the world, even if you've never left your living room.

I love reading album reviews: hearing a critic who knows lots about music, rating a band and talking about a CD. I find myself reading reviews of bands I know I hate or even ones I've never heard of, just so I can pick up some trivia about the band. But it's quite hard to describe music in terms of words. Reading a review is nothing compared to listening to an album. A paragraph on a page can't compare to the sounds, the ideas and the creativity held on that little silver disk. Reading should never be an alternative to experiencing the real world.

Because of my job as the pastor of a youth church, I often find myself doing assemblies and lunchtime clubs in schools. Recently, I was standing in a school corridor discussing music with a young person. When I asked her what kind of music she was into, she reeled of a long list of bands, most of whom I'd never heard of. But, not wanting to look un-cool, I stood there nodding and trying to make all the right noises until she said the name of a band I recognised from reading a review of them in *NME* magazine. I couldn't really remember whether the review had been good or not but I seemed to remember that the guy who produced the album had produced a couple of other albums that I'd heard of and that the guitarist from Primal Scream played a couple of songs on the CD. I made a positive sounding grunt and the girl asked if I liked them. Having just grunted I could hardly tell the truth, that the closest I'd come to hearing their music was reading a paragraph in a magazine. I let my pride get the best of me and I nodded, beginning to repeat the bits of information I'd read about the new CD. Luckily, the lunch bell rang and saved me from having to admit to my lack of knowledge.

Why is it that we are satisfied with reading a review? Why don't we want to experience things for ourselves?

We do this all the time where the Bible is concerned. We choose to read one of the million books written about Christianity rather than actually reading the Bible. Are you reading this book as a substitute for reading the Bible? Don't get me wrong, Christian books can help to unpack the things we don't understand, they can inspire us and make us excited but they can never be a substitute for the actual Word of God.

What was the last book you read? What is the most frequently read book on your shelf? Is it the Bible? I don't ask this to make you feel guilty but to get you to think about how important the Bible is to you. Is it something you pick up when life is tough, is it nothing but a coffee mat, or is it something that is so well worn through reading that you need to get another?

PURITY THROUGH THE TORAH

We've already talked a lot about purification leading to holiness, but in Jesus' time holiness also came through studying the Torah. The more someone studied the Torah, the more they became holy and righteous.

Noah was described by the writer of Genesis as being a righteous man, blameless among the people of his time (Gen. 6:9). One of the first men to ever meet Jesus as a child, is described in Luke 2:25 as being righteous and devout. For a Jew to be described as 'devout' would indicate that he prayed and studied the scriptures on a regular basis. For Jewish thinkers, the word 'righteous' is very similar to that of 'holy'. Righteousness is understood as conveying the idea of making good moral decisions and being without guilt or sin. It was believed that as a religious man studied the Torah and took in the knowledge on the page, the words brought them closer to God. Being closer to God makes us more holy or righteous.

This could almost be seen like taking in holiness by osmosis, with molecules of holiness moving from an area of high concentration to an area of low concentration,[17] from a holy God to unholy man.

Don't you agree that as we study the Bible we learn more about God and his ways?

TUNING OUR MINDS TO HIS

This Jewish understanding of becoming holier through reading God's word is perhaps something we should consider in the church. We tend to see studying the Scripture as something to help us make decisions in life or a way of trying to understand God. But perhaps something else happens within us as we read the Bible. Maybe as we read the Bible the very words on the page have the power to purify our thoughts. It says in 2 Timothy 3 that God's book has the power to 'rebuke and correct' us. But is it more than this? As we study the Bible and gain more understanding of God's ways, orientating our thoughts to his thoughts, do our minds become more like his?

If our mind becomes more like God's mind, surely we will become holier?

As I stood in that school corridor discussing a producer I barely knew anything about, I realised that I was spouting opinions that weren't even my own. Do I really think that he's a distinctive producer? Do I actually love the way he mixes the guitars and the drums to make a fresh sound? Suddenly, it became clear to me: I trusted the album reviewer of *NME* so much that I'd gradually started to absorb and articulate his views, without even realising.

When we read the Bible, our thoughts start to become more like our Creator's and less like those of this world.

Could it be that as we read God's book, we are becoming more holy as we orientate our minds to his ways?

We need to realise that studying the Bible is something all Christians should do. It's not just a book to be scrutinised to get a degree in theology. Neither is it a book we open when our life is a mess or we want to read something to make ourselves feel better. Neither is it just a rulebook or an instruction manual. The Bible is God's words for us, laying out the rescue plan for his people.

TUNING INTO A NEW WAY OF LIVING

I won't put forward an argument for how God's word is still applicable for today, although it can seem that way when we use it to look things up like a dictionary or an encyclopaedia. I don't deny that God can speak to us when we randomly open the Bible but it isn't a magic book or a fortune cookie. We need to be familiar and intimate with it. We need to understand what happened in the Old Testament, not just to help us understand the New Testament but because the Old Testament teaches us wisdom for our lives and knowledge about the character of God. We need to know what Jesus actually said, and why he said those things, and who he was saying them to. We need to know what happened after Jesus and how he changed things. We need to understand the context of the Bible so we can see how it is relevant for today. This book is vital.

Trying to live a holy life without knowing what God says on the subject is a little like playing a game when you don't know what the rules are. You know you're losing but you don't know why or how to win.

To be honest, I have tried to live according to the teaching I picked up in Sunday school. When my life started to become more complicated in my teenage years, I realised that the knowledge I'd gained though worksheets and games on a Sunday morning wasn't quite enough. When you're trying to navigate your way through issues such as sex, alcohol, friendships and pornography, stories about boats, snakes, whales and giants don't really scratch the itch.

Should I sleep with my girlfriend? Let's look at Noah and the Ark.

Is it wrong to smoke? Let's read about Jonah and the Whale.

My parents are splitting up and it's awful. Let's think about David and Goliath.

Don't get me wrong; these stories are not irrelevant to our lives at all. They all have vital knowledge about the character of God and are full of practical wisdom for our lives. But, we've got to know the whole story.

If we are to be God's holy people then we need to absorb God's thoughts by swimming around in his words.

As we dive into God's book, we start to see God's plans for us and we learn about his promises for us. As we read God's book we see what gifts he wants to lavish upon us. David wrote in Psalm 119, 'Your word is like a lamp for my feet and a light for my path' (v. 105).

Paul also understood what Scripture was created for when he was writing to his friends in Rome, 'everything that was written in the past was written to teach us, so that through endurance and the encouragement of the Scriptures we might have hope' (Rom. 15:4).

FILLING MY MIND WITH TONY

When I was at university, I would fall asleep with a *Tony Bennett live on MTV* CD playing in the background. It was a comfort thing, reminding me of the times I'd mucked around singing Tony Bennett songs with my friends from home. It's one of those long albums, with about twenty songs on, but I only knew about six of them.

One day, I was walking home from work when I realised that I was singing one of the tracks off the Tony Bennett CD that I didn't even know. I must have absorbed the lyrics when I was falling asleep each night. My mind was filling itself up with really un-cool, embarrassing songs without me even realising.

What would happen if we soaked ourselves in the Bible, absorbing the worship lyrics of the Psalms, the wisdom of Proverbs and the words of Jesus?

I have come to realise that a huge part of becoming holier is to do with what is going on in my mind. How can I call myself holy if I am thinking unholy thoughts?

We need to remember that holy thoughts do not suddenly appear or spring up like a plant from the ground. Our thoughts need to be nurtured. Our lives do not begin with holy thoughts but our holy thoughts begin with an experience of God's Holy Spirit. The holy thoughts become the theme that sounds within our minds and that grows its purity through time. The holy thoughts, for us as Christians, start when we interact with God, when we learn his ways and when we allow the words within his book to purify us. The gospel has a power that we too often don't understand.

2 Timothy 3:16–17 reads 'All Scripture is God-breathed and is useful for teaching, rebuking, correcting and training in righteousness, so that the man of God may be thoroughly equipped for every good work.'

Paul didn't write that 'all scripture is written by humans, but God chooses to use it anyway', which is sometimes the way we see it. The entire Bible is God-breathed, God created it in the same way he breathed life into Adam and Eve in the creation story. To use the image of God breathing it into life is like Paul saying that God gave birth to it. He nurtured it and gave it being and because of this, God's book is more authoritative then any other text ever written.

THE WORDS OF THE MASTER

One evening, I was travelling home on the train when I got chatting to the guy sitting in front of me. The guy introduced me to a copy of the Bible called a Red Letter Edition, which I found really helpful. The text was exactly the same as a normal Bible but the words of Jesus were printed in red. Suddenly it hit me that those words were the very words spoken by God here on earth. These words had life within them, spoken to real people at a real time.

These words were actually said by Jesus.

God's pure words.

On the train that day, I realised that I was reading the words of God. Yes, someone had written them down but these were the words he spoke.

They came out of the mouth of God.

Think about that for a moment; don't rush on to the next page.

The words of Matthew 5 are the very words that left God's mouth. Read it; try reading it out loud. Try reading it and imagine you were there hearing Jesus say them to you.

Please don't misunderstand what I am saying. The whole Bible is the word of God, God breathed it and he gave birth to it. But some of the words must be even more special because they were Jesus' words.

We need to hang onto these words, as intently as someone obsessed with a celebrity would listen to the words of their idol or like a little boy hangs onto the words of his Dad.

As a culture, we have lost the art of apprenticeship and masters. In the past, people didn't go to school after the age of twelve. Instead, they were signed up as an apprentice to a skilled worker such as a cobbler or a baker. The young boy (sorry girls, it was almost always guys) would learn the trade from his master, copying his actions and listening to his instructions carefully. We no longer have this art of hanging onto the words of masters, those who know more than us. But we need to relearn it. We need to hang on to the red letter words found in the gospels and learn from the man himself and not just what others say about him.

FIXING OUR EYES ON HIM

The other day, I was reading through the book of Hebrews when I came across a sentence that I'd completely forgotten existed: 'Therefore, holy brothers, who share in the heavenly calling, fix your thoughts on Jesus, the apostle and high priest whom we confess' (Heb. 3:1).

Fix your thoughts on Jesus could also be translated as fix your eyes on Jesus.

Straight away images of Jesus poured into my head. But this text doesn't tell us to fix our eyes on photos or paintings of Jesus. Images of Jesus can sometimes be useful in helping us to focus on him but the author of Hebrews isn't talking about this. Neither is he saying that we need to look at relics (things that were around at the time of Jesus and linked with his life). So, what does the writer of this letter mean when he says we need to fix our thoughts on Jesus?

He means we need to study, hang onto and fix our thoughts on Jesus' teaching and ministry. It means reading the red letters in the Gospels of Matthew, Mark, Luke and John and absorbing the words of Christ into our hearts and minds.

When I was younger, I'd occasionally go to work with my dad on a Saturday. Dad is an electrician and he used to work on many different jobs like burglar alarms, lighting, schools and shops. But, the most exciting part of his job was every year doing the Christmas lights in Leeds town centre.

Once, Dad took me with him whilst he put up the Christmas lights in town. He explained what he was doing as he went along and I remember being absolutely fascinated. I watched what he was doing and tried to match it up with what he was saying. I loved it. We need to be like that with Jesus, listening to his words with all of our attention and trying to match them up with our lives.

CHRISTIANOS AND MATHETES

Did you know that the Greek word *christianos* or 'Christian' is only used in the Bible three times?

> Now it was in Antioch that the disciples were first called Christians (Acts 11:26).

> Then Agrippa said to Paul, "Do you think that in such a short time you can persuade me to be a Christian?"(Acts 26:28)

> However, if you suffer as a Christian, do not be ashamed, but praise God that you bear that name (1 Pet. 4:16).

Before people were commonly known as Christians, they were known as followers of The Way (see Appendix) or as disciples. The word 'disciple' is used around two hundred and seventy times within the first five books of the New Testament. The Greek word used for disciple is *mathetes*, which can also be translated as 'a learner' or 'an apprentice'. The word 'disciple' is used because we are meant to be people who are learning and studying the ways of God. A person studying and learning is allowed to make mistakes and do things wrong.

My son Isaac is learning how to do many things, such as not to pinch people, how to articulate his thoughts, to eat tidily and to use a potty. He makes a fair few mistakes but it's OK because he's learning.

There was a terrible incident in our kitchen recently, involving our son, a potty and a lot of wet wipes. It wasn't pretty but we accepted it. If he were twenty-one and still doing it then there might be a problem but he's two and learning to be an independent person.

Little children don't learn how to behave by sitting in a classroom, they learn by trying new things and getting things wrong. You wouldn't try to teach a classroom of two-year-olds theories on how to use a potty or how to dress themselves. A child learns by being in the world and that's exactly how Jesus taught his followers.

We need to realise the Bible isn't just something for quiet times, cell groups and theological colleges. The Bible is meant to be explored, discovered and studied in our lives. We don't have to keep our Bible studies intellectual and theoretical; the Bible is made for our messy, busy, crazy lives.

The word *mathetes* can also mean 'doer'. We are to fix our eyes on Jesus but that doesn't just mean thinking about it in a quiet room, it means working out how it fits into our world. Paul stressed this when he wrote to James: 'Do not merely listen to the word and so deceive yourselves. Do what it says' (James 1:22).

As *mathetes* we are called to fix our eyes on Jesus and meditate on his words so that we might come to know the one who blesses us and through osmosis become more like him. Not so that we might think of ourselves as holy but so that we might do what it says. Holiness isn't simply about trying to reach a state of holiness where our heads are in the clouds, it's about knowing the Creator more so that we might do what he says, being his hands and feet on earth.

Being God's representatives.

LIVING IT OUT

- How have you seen God working in you when you have spent time reading the Bible? Has there been a time where he has significantly changed you through it?

- We can only be changed by something with which we significantly interact. How can you allow more time for this to happen with the Bible?

- Have you ever spent time just reading the words of Jesus? Why not read the Sermon on the Mount in Matthew 5? What is significantly different to this teaching that Jesus brings and the teaching you hear in church or by other Christians?

- What do you fill your mind with? Try making a list of the top five things you read, listen to and watch. How is God represented in this list? Is he represented at all? Think about how this list could be used to damage the renewal of your mind of which the Bible speaks.

- How can you inspire other Christians to study their Bible more? Is there something that you are already doing that could help others to find hope and renewal in the Bible?

FURTHER READING

How to Read the Bible for All Its Worth by Gordon D. Fee and Douglas Stuart is an inspirational book with regard to getting into the Bible.

Nick Page's *The Bible Book* is also a helpful study aid for new readers.

DAVE | 09

JACOB TO JESUS, ESAU TO HEROD

The Gospel of Matthew opens with a list of those who had played their part in God's story in the Old Testament. Almost like a recap at the beginning of the third part of a film trilogy or the start of the second season of a TV series. This list is a family tree running right from Abraham who fathered Isaac, who then fathered Jacob, down to Jesus.

Chapter 2 then begins 'After Jesus was born in Bethlehem in Judea, during the time of King Herod' (v. 1). If you imagine that in this gospel Jesus is seen as the hero, then King Herod is clearly the oppressor and the evil tyrant. Jesus comes from the family line of Jacob, the one who stole the family blessing, and although we are not told it, the Jews at the time would know that King Herod came from the family of Esau, the hairy one who lost the blessing.

Jacob to Jesus, Esau to Herod.

For a Jewish reader Matthew is starting to set the scene for a fantastic story. This story starts with us finding out that the two opening characters have a previous history, a history where Jacob and Esau fought over who was going to hold the power of the family kingdom. The backdrop to this story is that of two kings fighting over a new kingdom, one with all earthly power and wealth and one with all heavenly power and wealth. Two kings, one humble and one not. One born in opulence and one born in poverty.

King Herod, half Jewish and half Edomite, was a fearless king who did anything to keep power over his kingdom. His power over people came from fear and violence and he was seriously mentally unstable. It is well known that King Herod massacred those in his way, and the history books document that Herod killed his wives[18] and many of his children.[19] It is thought that he did this because he was suspicious and paranoid of his family; Herod believed that they wanted him dead for his money and power.

Herod wished to show his power and authority by building monuments other rulers could not afford or didn't have the power to. Herod taxed the Jewish people on top of Rome's tax, thereby reducing them to a situation of profound poverty merely so he could build his marvellous kingdom. Herod built temples, including the huge Second Temple in Jerusalem, amphitheatres, theatres, racecourses and seaports out in the sea. One seaport, called *Caesarea Maritima*, was on marshland so Herod decided to use concrete – historians are still amazed he managed to get hold of this material.[20] This seaport was created and dedicated to the Roman Caesar so that Herod would remain in his good books and nothing more. Herod also built a palace on the side of a mountain, *Masada*, and with it water and sewage systems, huge baths and enough storage for figs and dates to last a lifetime.

Knowing that at some point in the future people might attack Jerusalem, Herod decided to build a fortress between Jerusalem and his home of Edom that he could run to if needed. Herod chose a location to build a fortress but there wasn't a mountain in that location so he had his own mountain shipped in. Don't ask me where he found an unused mount but trust me there is now one missing somewhere. On this he created a palace, creatively called Herodium, which he fitted with large bathing pools, steam rooms, meeting rooms and banqueting halls.

He built with such massive stones that even today we don't know how the slaves moved them. He was an oppressor who did things simply so that he could impress the world. Some historians believe he was probably one of the richest men in the world of all time.

In Matthew 21:21, as Jesus stood on the Mount of Olives and looked out from Jerusalem, he would have clearly been able to see Herod's Herodium. Turning to his disciples he tells them that if they have faith, they 'can say to this mountain, "Go, throw yourself into the sea," and it will be done.' If we understand the geography, suddenly Jesus is talking about a specific artificial mountain, a symbol of oppressive power, squandered money and a yearning for a lifestyle of gluttony with no humility in sight. Could it be that Jesus was commenting on what is acceptable and what isn't, and that power by wealth is oppressive? For Jesus the gospel is about restoration, freedom and liberation and this can only happen through our humility and his.

The original Jewish readers and disciples would have understood Jesus' reference to the sea to be a reference to the 'abyss' or, as we might say, hell. Is Jesus really saying to his disciples, 'Hey people, do you realise that with my power and my strength, you will be able to tell the mighty powers of this world to drop dead?' and 'Guys, you have the power in me to bring down the evil of this world and throw it into the pits of hell'?

Jesus was the king of humility and Herod the king of pride. Jesus' kingdom was going to be built not by the sword nor oppression but by undermining those who cause suffering in the world. Jesus' idea of authority is almost an upside-down authority compared to the world's idea. Jesus' death is a perfect example of this. The oppressive powers tried to hold Jesus down but in fact he used this position of apparent weakness to undermine the whole system and seize a different type of power.

Our God is the God who brings down human powers, human oppressors, human dictators and time has shown that it only takes the faith and humility of one person to turn things around.

IT'S ALL ABOUT THE GUY ON THE STAGE

When visiting a leadership conference I arrived just as the keynote speaker was telling the crowd how fantastic and perfect his church was. He told us that he had almost five thousand people each week in services where they see people healed from all illnesses, diseases and deformities including the HIV virus. Freshly seated, I could not believe what was coming out of this guy's mouth. He boasted about his giving being so much that they give millions to the poor, that they serve Starbucks coffee and muffins at the back of his church for free and that he tours the world with his international ministry.

IT'S 'NOT' ALL ABOUT THE GUY ON THE STAGE

I can't tolerate ministers who 'big up' their church to make others think how amazing their leadership is. I'm sure that you have met people at school, college or work who are proud of themselves but still seem to ooze false humility. Books have been written, films have been made, and TV shows beamed to every TV showing the hypocrisy of some church leaders.

You have to admit, if you have ever had the pleasure of watching Christian TV channels, there are some American ones where a finely polished presenter stands preaching the gospel under the banner of humility. Although eventually this image always comes apparent, just in the same way other sins are uncovered in due time, the sin of pride is no different.

As I sat in the room with hundreds of other church leaders clapping and cheering it got me thinking. What is humility really and did Jesus ever boast about how crazy his ministry was?

Sat at the lunch table, a few hours later, with a group of people I had only just met, they spoke of how fantastic the speaker had been that morning and how inspired he made them feel.

How inspired 'he' made them feel.

I sat in my seat desperately trying to articulate what was going through my mind thinking 'How inspired "he" made you feel. I'm sorry but isn't it Jesus the one who should inspire us? Not some guy telling us how great his church was because surely it's Jesus' Church, isn't it?'

Suddenly a woman on my right asked me where I was from, and what church I led. Still frustrated by the conversation, defensively I answered, 'I help lead a small church in North London.'

Underplaying everything we do as a church, I suddenly felt God poke me. It was almost like God spoke to me and said, 'Are you selling my church short?'

It was as though I was being falsely modest about what we were doing. God is being so good to my church at the moment, we are reaching people who would never normally be reached by regular churches and I'm playing God's work down. Suddenly I felt as bad as if I was the guy on the stage boasting about the size of my church like teenage boys boasting about their manhoods.

IT'S MY FATHER'S CHURCH

Sat that night in my dull 1960s decorated hotel room with only three TV channels, my mind turned back to the preacher and the lunch earlier. If I am desiring to be a follower of my heavenly Father who sees me as a prince and is wanting to bless me with his presence, then how do I deal with pride (the sin of wanting to 'big myself up') and the problem of being falsely modest and denying what God is doing? This got me thinking and then led me to the New Testament.

Paul, in the book of Corinthians, says all believers are members of the body of Christ, which in turn makes up his church. Paul writes, 'the body is a unit, though it is made up of many parts; and though all its parts are many, they form one body. So it is with Christ' (1 Cor. 12:12).

As a member of this body, I believe that I am someone who has been given gifts by God to use within his church. I am creative, enjoy teaching and preaching, am gifted in evangelism and, if pushed, can lead worship from time to time. For me to say to someone that I don't have any gifts or to even say that they aren't real gifts surely undermines the gifts that have been given to me by God?

The reason that I have been given gifts is nothing to do with anything that I can do or achieve by myself; I only have then because my Father has been willing to give them in the first place and they are given to us for the sake of the Body of Christ, the wider church. We also need to realise that if we don't exercise the gift to its utmost we are being falsely modest and downplaying the gift giver.

Correct modesty leads us to realise that God is the supplier of gifts and he wants us to use them for his ministry. Therefore we can be bold with our actions, trusting in God and using the gifts to grow his church for his and only his glory. Surely as Christians we need to be excited about the gifts of others and seek those that God has given us? We need to be proud of the gift giver and not that we are the ones who have been given them.

Paul writes in 2 Corinthians 10:17 that those of us who want to boast should be allowed to do so, but only boasting in Christ Jesus.

A LITTLE MORE FROM DAVID

Back in chapter three we looked at the fantastic story of David and Goliath which happened years before he spotted Bathsheba in the bath. David was nothing more than a small fluffy-haired shepherd spending many of his waking hours on the hills with sheep playing his harp. Not really the image of a ruling type. I would like us to go back again and dig a little deeper into the story.

After forty days David was sent by his dad, Jesse, to take bread and a nice spread of cheese to the commander of the unit. So not only was David a harp player, he was also a cheese delivery boy. As David made his delivery, Goliath, the Philistine champion, stepped up to the battle line shouting his usual line of abuse and, as usual, no one was going forward.

So David steps up to the task. Many would say that David was wildly over-confident and stupid to even compare his training in fighting wild animals with Goliath. Nevertheless David is given permission by Saul and steps out with nothing but his slingshot and a few polished stones.

Goliath steps up to his challenger with his eyes wide open; he is nothing but a boy and a handsome harp-playing cheese-carrying one at that. Stepping up to Goliath David calls out to him saying

> You come against me with sword and spear and javelin, but I come against you in the name of YHVH Almighty, the God of the armies of Israel, whom you

> have defied. This day YHVH will hand you over to me,
> and I'll strike you down and cut off your head. Today
> I will give the carcasses of the Philistine army to the
> birds of the air and the beasts of the earth, and the
> whole world will know that there is a God in Israel. All
> those gathered here will know that it is not by sword
> or spear that YHVH saves; for the battle is YHVH's,
> and he will give all of you into our hands (1 Sam.
> 17:45–47).

David, sounding even more over-confident than before,
was rapidly attacked by the Philistine so he ran quickly
towards him with sling spinning in his hand. David
reaches into his little man bag carrying his stones, slips
it into his sling, slings it and as we read earlier strikes
Goliath on the forehead.

Hole in one!

GOAL!

With the pebble sinking into Goliath's over-large forehead he falls onto the ground: to which David's
response is to chop off his head.

EGO OR CONFIDENCE

Was David arrogant or was it just that he was aware of the
gifting that God had blessed him with? If David had
underplayed his gifting that morning the events of the day
would probably have been very different. The nine-foot
maniac would have probably trounced the Israelites leaving David's people open to be taken over by the Philistines.

David only gets the job done because he speaks out
about his gifting. Does this mean David was not humble
but an outspoken cocky teenager? Or does humility go
much deeper than that?

While packing up after church a few months ago one of the young people I mentor was chatting to me about this very topic. Turning to me, the young guy, with a cheeky grin on his face, said 'Well, of course Cris, humility is confidence correctly placed in God.' I hate it when teenagers I am meant to be leading and training get one over me and get something that I take hours to say in a nutshell! It certainly humbles me.

Humility is confidence correctly placed in God.

I love it, it's so simple. We are humble when we place everything we are, everything we have and everything we will have in God. This moves us away from seeing 'stuff' as ours to seeing 'our stuff' as something that God lends us. No longer are we in full control but now we are in God's control.

CONFIDENCE CORRECTLY PLACED IN GOD

It seems to me that those who are really humble don't have any idea they really are. It's just something about them as a person. Then there are people like me who have to try and work at what it means and how to become more humble.

Humility is confidence correctly placed in God; with King David we find out that true humility is actually confidence correctly placed in a God who wants us to succeed in growing the kingdom and becoming wise strong leaders.

Humility is seen in the Catholic Church as one of the seven heavenly virtues[21] to be sought after by all followers of Christ. We also need to remember that humility is a part of the character of God alongside generosity, mercy, grace and forgiveness.

GOD WOKE AND DID SOMETHING

God woke (if he sleeps that is and I can't theologically back that up) two thousand years ago and knew that he had to do something about the amount of oppression, imprisonment and cruelty in the world. God knew that the worship of the people was not reaching the mark and that the sacrifices and burnt offerings were worthless.

If you were a celebrity with all the money in the world at your fingertips and you wanted for nothing, why would you choose to live like those who have nothing? Why would you choose to do real work, choose to see people fighting for life, choose to see people begging and choose to see people broken and desperate? Would you not just stay in your little mansion on the hill with indoor swimming pool and wall-mounted TV?

The strange thing is *YHVH* the Creator of the Universe, the God who can do anything and create anything chose on that day to step down from his throne room and become human. Moving into the neighbourhood he was born in the lower level of a Jewish home where the animals lived. God humbled himself to become one of those he created; he then grew as a Jewish boy learning the family trade. God walked the earth as a human for thirty years before he even preached his first sermon. In those decades he would have seen everything a regular human would see up to their thirtieth birthday. He would have seen death of family members, which probably would include his adopted father Joseph's death. He would have suffered the embarrassments of puberty, heard his voice drop and supported people who were deeply troubled. God was real; feeling pain, anger and upset. Have you ever thought about how much God gave up to make that move? Have you ever thought about the things he would have started doing that he hadn't done before?

Jesus, God in Flesh, then dips further into humanity when he faces the cross for all mankind. Paul writing to the church in Philippi says that 'Being found in appearance as a man, he humbled himself and became obedient to death – even death on a cross!' (Phil. 2:8).

How much more of an example of humility do we need to see before we realise that this is something we need to be striving for. Orientation to the Father, recognising his mighty forgiveness, his amazing love, his fantastic protection and his humility should move us to see that all of this is about holiness and that we need to be becoming more like him.

BECOMING MORE LIKE HIM

We see humility and suffering going hand in hand in Matthew in chapter 23, 'for whoever exalts himself will be humbled, and whoever humbles himself will be exalted' (Mt. 23:12).

It's almost like God's gravity has the opposite pull to that of the world. Being proud of ourselves is the message of the media-centred, money-making world we inhabit. The world says we should strive to be people who are admired, people who achieve mighty things, and people who are powerful. God's gravity says that we should strive to be peaceful, living lives of servants and not masters, longing to see the poor become rich in him so that we might then be exalted to what God sees as mighty.

THERE WAS NO CHANCE

A few years ago I organised a trip to the local swimming pool for a group of twenty-five young people at my church.

There were about two hundred people in the pool. Until this point, as a leader, it felt so good knowing that my young people saw me as a hero: someone who was strong in their faith, that had a mind like one of the great theologians of the past and who could answer any one of their deep theological troubles. It also felt good to think that they respected me and looked up to me as their leader, some of them probably thought that I could walk on water.

When we arrived at the pool edge, half of my young people paced it to the extremely high diving board and then jumped off, while I was content to bob in the water. After they had jumped three times or so one by one they came and started coaxing me to jump too. After quite a lot of persuading I started to climb the twenty-metre high diving board ladder. Reaching the halfway point I began to be nervous about the height. When I reached the top my stomach had butterflies because I could not believe how far away the water was. Suddenly my brain went into overload.

Surely I could die?

What happened if I land on the water wrongly and my belly splits open?

What if I hit my head on the bottom?

What if I belly flop it?

There was no way this was going to happen; there was no way I could jump. I started to think that maybe I could climb down giving the excuse I had something in my eye or that I had just remembered that the doctor had told me not to jump off high things because of my bad leg. Looking out from the top of the diving board I noticed that all twenty-five young people were in the pool waiting for my body to launch from this health and safety nightmare. 'Jump, jump, jump' they started to chant, soon the whole pool was chanting too all two hundred of them. The chant soon changed to 'Jump, Rogers, Jump'.

Minutes passed as I stood on the edge of the diving board. By now the lifeguards were joining in trying to get me to jump, as the queue for the suicidal fall had started to grow. Deciding that it would be better to lose face than a limb I climbed down the long ladder of shame to a chorus of boos. Reaching the bottom I walked with my head down around the pool to sit on the edge with my young people.

The following week I stood in one of the local high schools teaching about sex in a classroom of about thirty teenagers. Just as the lesson had started a lad at the back put up his hand and asked . . .

'Are you the freak who was too scared to jump off the diving board?'

Walking down the corridor of the school three girls and a guy started shouting 'Jump, jump, jump' at me. I was horrified and very embarrassed and had no idea how I could ever regain my street-cred. It was then that it hit me; I was too worried about what these young people thought. I needed to be humbled. Maybe I needed to lose my street-cred to realise that it was something I was longing for from people I worked with. I was brought down several pegs that weekend; I no longer walked on water, which was very releasing. The strange thing was, from that point on I suddenly was real in a way that my young people liked. I wasn't the youth leader who they thought was perfect, but now I was a real guy who struggled with the same things that they struggled with.

HUMILITY AND GROWTH

Paul in the book of Philippians saw humiliating circumstances as an opportunity to grow in humility and trust in the Father more. He wrote

> I know what it is to be in need, and I know what it is to
> have plenty. I have learned the secret of being content in
> any and every situation, whether well fed or hungry,
> whether living in plenty or in want, I can do everything
> through him who gives me strength (Phil. 4:12–13).

Growing in humility is about realizing that nothing is about us, but everything is about God. Have you ever had a humiliating experience? Has it helped you grow in humility, or did you just strive to make sure you didn't lose face? It's a question worth thinking about.

Sitting in that conference hearing the preacher talk about his church really got under my skin, but me underplaying God's work in my life is just as bad. There needs to be a balance where we are able to get excited by God's good gifts but also are humble enough to know that it is nothing to do with us.

The question I have been thinking about deep in my soul has been 'Would I be any different if I had been asked to talk about the things I have seen God do in my church?' Could it be that his attitude in some strange way had made me see a little of him in me and that it was this that I had hated?

The writer of the book of Proverbs knew that pride will bring down any strong godly leader. Why not spend some time looking at these two proverbs and spend time praying that God will aid you to be wise in making sure that you only pride yourself in him and nothing else? Pray that God would capture you with his gravity's pull and not the world's.

> When pride comes, then comes disgrace, but with
> humility comes wisdom (Prov. 11:2).
> Pride only breeds quarrels, but wisdom is found in those
> who take advice (Prov. 13:10).

LIVING IT OUT

- Have you seen confidence correctly placed in God lived out by anyone you know? What did it look like? If not, what do you think it would look like?

- How can we work out if someone is living for his or her ego or with confidence in God? What would you say were the differences between these two ways of living?

- Has there been a time where your ego has taken over something you were doing? Can you see at what point this happened or how this happened? What can you do to make sure this happens less often in the future?

- If nothing is about us but everything is about God, how does this make us live? How would this affect the way we see our possessions or the way we use money?

- Jesus presents to us this image of a man humbling himself to the point where others are more important than his own life. Can you see any possibility of you becoming that humble? Many of us would say no – if this is the case what do you think is holding so many of us back?

FURTHER READING

C.J. Mahaney's *Humility* is a superb book on this issue of Jesus and his humility and is very inspirational.
Living the Cross Centred Life also by C.J. Mahaney looks at how we practically live out the humility found on the cross in our day-to-day living.

NAKED | 10

THAT VERY LARGE SHOP IN LEEDS

Have you ever been carefully watched by someone?

Once, when I was younger, I was out shopping in Leeds city centre with Andy, a friend of mine, when we decided to go into a certain very large department store on the high street. We spent quite a bit of time wandering around the store looking at things we would love to buy but then talking about how extortionate the prices were. £2.15 for a tin of space-baked beans! After some time, Andy turned to me and asked had I realised we were being followed. Slightly freaking out at this I turned to see a very stern-looking security guard stood only metres away trying to look incognito behind the tinned banana chunks and chillied apple cakes.

Aware that the security guard was following us, I decided to have a little fun with him. I started to pick up items from the shelves and move them around the store. You can't be arrested for moving stock can you? I moved a nice silk shirt into the house and home section, a large standard lamp into the chilled goods section and a packet of space food into the men's underwear section. As I turned round the tall security guard was now only a metre away and still being really bad at pretending he wasn't there. This guy seriously needed some training on tailing people without being seen.

I suddenly had an idea: how close could I get to the door of the store without being arrested? I know from my short time in retail you can't arrest someone unless they leave the store with the goods. At this point I ditched Andy and decided this was something I needed to do alone, this was something I needed to do for me, this was almost like a rite of passage for me, boy becomes man, kind of thing. It wasn't really fair to Andy to involve him; plus, I didn't think it would look good for him if it went wrong and we ended up down the nick for theft.

Reaching out for the first thing that I could find I clutched to me the item that I was going to take with me to either my arrest or the most fun thing I was ever going to do (that weekend). Before I tell you what the item was I need you to realise something. This item says nothing about me, or my sexuality, I don't normally try to buy things like this and I would not have taken it if I had been in another department. Please understand this really does not need to be mentioned after you have read this book, my mum and dad have no need to know, trust me please.

The item that I had in my hand was a salmon pink bra. There was no turning back, this was the item I was going to use for my experiment. Some people do experiments on cats and bells; some do experiments on splitting the atom; I do experiments on salmon pink bras and how far you can fling them in departments stores.

I was on the second floor and I started to make my way to the escalator closely being followed by the security guard. By the time I stepped onto the escalator there now were two guards behind me. Stepping off the escalator I saw two more security guys on my right and left. I started to run towards the revolving door on the bottom floor, now with two behind me, two on my sides and at this moment with two huge guys making their way quite fast towards the door. I started sprinting as I approached the spinning door and with one last look over my shoulder, I knew it was now or never as the six men were only moments away. Holding the salmon pink bra in my right hand I threw it to my right just before I got near the alarm sensors. Jumping into the revolving door I stepped out from it and give it a little flick so that it now was spinning far too fast for anyone to ever get in it. I then ran up the high street knowing what it was like to be carefully watched.

REAL PEOPLE

Have you ever been that carefully watched for something, a time when people have got their eyes all over you?

Have you ever been that carefully watched by your friends because of your faith?

When I was investigating nudism for my talk on 'What does it mean to be a Christian?' I became interested in the reason nudism was so appealing to some people. After finding the fig leaf forum I came to realise that the attraction was allowing people to see you as you were created, warts and all. Members of the website talked about loving the freedom of not having to dress to impress but being able to be people who were free from the bondage of consumerism and materialism.

Many of us wear masks. Not the party or Darth Vader type of mask but masks that cover up who we are. We wear clothing, have our hair in a style and wear make-up that tells people who we want to be.

I have recently joined the myspace.com phenomena with thousands of others. I wanted to create my myspace in a way that would tell the world, this is who I am. It is so interesting to see what pictures people choose to put on their space. Never do you see their bad hair days, or shots of people with zits. People also have created new names for themselves so that they are almost someone else while online, a cyber version of their real self.

Have you recognised the desperation within our culture to present a perfect person with no defects? Do you do this?

Nudism is poles apart from myspace. Nudists are people trying to be countercultural, presenting to the world the bad hair day whereas myspace is creating a cyber mask. Nudism got me thinking, surely this is what God wants for us. Let me make it clear God wants us to wear clothes, I am not promoting nudism. But there is something about wearing your heart on your sleeve, not dressing yourself up, being willing to show the world who you really are, that is very godly.

BEING CAREFULLY WATCHED

Let me tell you a story about rabbi Jesus, found in Luke 14.

One holy day Jesus was invited for Sunday lunch at the local, and very highly respected, Jewish leader's house. While he was there he was being carefully watched. Everyone sat chatting, eating and drinking wine, when a man with dropsy entered the house and stood in front of Jesus. Dropsy is basically water retention, which means that you swell up. Imagine Violet Beauregarde in *Charlie and the Chocolate Factory* when she eats the gum and swells up to look like a blueberry.

Jesus, already knowing the answer to his question, turned to ask the Jewish leader and the other guests who were experts in the Jewish law found in the Torah, 'Is it wrong to heal a man on a holy day?'

The Jewish experts, being experts, knew that it was a major sin to do any work on a holy day. This command stemmed right back to the Ten Commandments and would have definitely included healing someone who was sick.

There were so many laws in Jewish tradition by this point, that the rabbis had come up with a way of trying to decide which were more important when it looked as though two laws were in contradiction. This was called heavier and lighter; they would take two commands and decided which was more important (heavier) than the other (lighter).

Leviticus 22:3 would have indicated to the teachers of the law that healing on the Sabbath would be a sin. However Jesus knew that Leviticus 19:18 commanded you to love your neighbour as yourself. This command implies that not to love your neighbour is not to worship YHVH. Jesus had weighed up the two commands and deemed 19:18 heavier than 22:3, contradicting the traditional Jewish conclusion to the question.

Believing that it was wrong to heal, the experts and teachers of the Torah remained silent and watched Jesus carefully. Jesus promptly took hold of the man, healed him and sent him home.

Jesus turned to them again and asked 'If you had a son who fell down a well on a holy day would you not immediately pull him out?' The Jewish experts and teachers had nothing to say, but they still did not take their eyes off him.

Jesus was carefully watched because of his behaviour. The Jewish leaders were hanging onto every one of his words desperate to catch him out and trip him up. On many occasions they asked Jesus difficult questions to trick him, but he was fully aware of the games that they were playing and did not play along. He was constantly silencing his critics with acts of love.

Wherever Jesus went he was carefully watched because of his fresh interpretation on the Torah and his radical new view of who were the Jews' neighbours. Jesus also hung out with the wrong crowds, he spoke to prostitutes, had dinner with tax collectors (who were hated more than modern-day traffic wardens) and he touched the sick, including those who were demon possessed. Jesus acted and lived in a radical new way.

RADICAL JESUS

Let us spend some time looking at how radical Jesus was. Back in chapter six we examined the story of the Good Samaritan (Luke 10:15) and I want us to go back there for a moment because there is more going on in that story than first meets the eye.

The Jewish expert who came to Jesus was trying to test him; the expert's question wasn't quite what we think he is asking. When asked 'Who is my neighbour?' he was referring to a debate that had been going for some time. It was believed at the time that a Jew's neighbours were in fact other Jews around them and not those who they didn't like or get on with. The expert is essentially asking are you one of those rabbis who are liberal enough to believe these sinners are our neighbours?

So Jesus tells the story of the man travelling from Jerusalem to Jericho, who had been attacked by robbers. He had been stripped and left half dead. If you had a stranger standing in front of you and you wanted to know where they were from, you would probably do one of two things. The first would be to check out their clothing; is it western clothing or eastern clothing; does it fit within any culture you know? Secondly you could check out their voice; listen to their accent. So when Jesus presents this man to the listeners as naked and half dead, what Jesus is saying is we don't know anything about this man, we don't know if he is rich or poor, we don't know what he did for work and we don't know if he is married or single. All we are left to presume is that he is Jewish.

The story that Jesus told was not a new story and had been told by other rabbis for centuries. In the Jewish version of the story, three men pass by the 'thought-to-be-dead' man. First a priest, then the Levite and then, in their story, a Jewish lay person who was simply a regular Jewish person who would have been spending time serving in the temple. The point of their story was about being ritually clean as we looked at earlier.

Jesus tells the listeners about the first two men walking by and then moves onto the third man. You can imagine all the listeners waiting for Jesus to tell the story of how a Jewish layman helps the injured man, but Jesus creates a twist in the story. In this telling of the story Jesus tells them that some time passed and a Samaritan man and his donkey comes by.

We need to understand some of the cultural background to what Jesus is saying. The Jews did not associate with Samaritans due to a dispute over where God could be worshipped. The Jews believed that the only place that you could worship God was in the temple found in Jerusalem, whereas the Samaritans believed it was Mount Gerizim. Jews hated the Samaritans; they even had points in their worship when they would pray that God would curse the Samaritan people.

In one Jewish book around in Jesus' time called *Mishna Seveth* the writer says that the person who eats the bread of a Samaritan is like the one who eats the flesh of pigs. In their culture a pig was given the same regard we would give rats: they were dirty and carried diseases.

The Jewish teacher Ben Sira, who lived two hundred years before Jesus, said that there were two nations he detested and the third is not a nation at all, the inhabitants of Mount Sear and those stupid people of Shechem. Shechem was where the Samaritans lived.

For the Jews it had become a racist hate. Have you ever hated someone that much that you would pray a curse onto them?

As the Samaritan arrived, Jesus says that he took deep compassion on the dying man. He bound up his wounds and used oil and wine on his cuts. Do you notice what Jesus does there? Not only had he said that the Jewish men put worship above the dying man, he now even pokes at them further. The Samaritan man uses oil and wine for medical use; these two elements were used everyday in the Jewish temple for worship. Jesus comments on the Jewish men's priorities and then shows how what they used for worship (which would have been seen as sacred things) is then used on the half-dead man. Love, care and concern are greater acts here for Jesus than the worship in the temple. Jesus is commenting here on how the social action of being a servant is in itself worship.

These are the comments that made people watch Jesus and because he challenged deeply held beliefs, they wanted to try and twist his words.

Are you carefully watched because you are being different? Because you are doing acts of love?

Jesus calls us as Christians to live lives that are open, free for people to see what is going on in our hearts, to be almost 'spiritual nudists'. There is absolutely no point saying that you are a follower of Jesus if your behaviour undermines your words. Our lives need to be naked, willing at any time to be countercultural. Jesus knew that healing on the holy day was seen as breaking the Old Testament Law, but he also knew that to not allow God's love to flood into the life of the man with dropsy was an even greater sin.

SALT

Like Jesus our holiness should cause others to want to watch us and see what is different about us. Another image Jesus used was to call us to be salt and light in the darkness of the world. Salt had a number of different uses within Jesus' culture, compared to today. We put salt on food especially fish and chips, to make it taste nice and bring out the flavour. There were two very distinctive uses of salt in Galilee. Rock salt was readily available due to the high salt content in the Dead Sea, which gains its saltiness from the earth and rock it covers. When people went behind their homes to go to the loo they would dig a hole and then place large chunks of sea salt on the waste to stop flies getting to it. The salt would also help in breaking down the waste and act like an antiseptic; this type of salt was called the 'salt of the earth'.

The other way it was used was in cooking. People would use dome ovens made of dried or baked mud. They would then mix the salt with dried donkey waste, which was a very common fuel and is still used today in some areas. Because of the salt there was a chemical reaction that made the mixture burn much more effectively. Not only did it burn brighter but also hotter and longer.

Like the salt we use today it still lost its salty taste and its usefulness if it became damp or was not used for a long time, so was thrown out – a point Jesus mentions when he calls us as Christians to be like the salt of the earth, 'You are the salt of the earth. But if the salt loses its saltiness, how can it be made salty again? It is no longer good for anything, except to be thrown out and trampled by men' (Mt. 5:13).

As Jesus' followers, he calls us to do several things. Firstly, to be like an antiseptic to the 'crap' we find in the world we are in. Secondly, we need to mix with the donkey droppings, which is the sinful world around us, and still keep our distinctive Christian salty identity. We need to allow our mixing with the world to show Christ's love brighter, stronger and for longer. If we claim to be holy but it doesn't show, then there has to be something going wrong with our holiness chip. We need to see that the people we are becoming have eternal implications on those around us.

Life isn't about what we have or what masks we are able to wear but is about the eternal things; love, joy, peace, feeding the hungry and clothing the poor; and being merciful, humble and forgiving. So many people hang on to the lie that this life needs to be lived because this is all we have. However, we need to realise that this place isn't all there is with nothing more, but that this world is only for now and there is an eternal one to come. Once we realise that then we can truly start to live, be free, be holy and be spiritually nude.

It says in Romans 6:23 that the cost of sinning is death but through Jesus we have eternal life. The word the writer uses for eternal life is the Greek word *aionios* which would be better translated as living the unending real life. A life that is more real than anything we have ever experienced.

FORGIVE AND MOVE ON

I was recently talking to a police officer about a young person that I had been working with at church. This guy had done some really silly things to try and destroy the work God was doing though the church community. When the police officer asked me what I was planning to do with him my answer was 'forgive him and move on'.

This blew the police officer's mind. 'Surely you are going to ban him or make him pay for the damage?' he asked. The truth is I hadn't planned to ban him and neither was I going to ask him to pay for any of the damage he had caused. For me this simply wasn't the way Jesus worked, never did we see him trying to get one over someone or get back at them.

If this world is it and there is nothing else, forgiveness does not make sense: to get one over on someone or get your own back makes much more sense. This comment of forgiving the young guy obviously had stuck in the mind of the officer because he brought it back up in conversation several times, the idea of allowing someone to be forgiven, so that they could be free from the sin with which they had trapped themselves, was mind-blowing for someone whose only focus was this world.

Because of these words of forgiveness I was able to talk to the officer for almost an hour about how Jesus worked, what were his values and what were his ways. The officer sat silently for a time as he looked blankly at me, this just wasn't what he expected from a Christian. He had spoken to other Christians he had met who were quite happy to get their own back on someone for the things that they had had done to them.

Our behaviour speaks volumes about what we believe about Christ. Even if you aren't able to have a conversation about your faith with people, simply your actions are seen, even the small things.

HOLINESS IS EVANGELISTIC

Paul wrote to the Thessalonians saying that we should live lives that get on with the reality of life so that we might win the respect of others.[22]

Suddenly I get something I've never seen before. Holiness in fact can be used as an evangelistic tool drawing others closer to the message of the cross and its redemption through our own behaviour. If we are holy as Christ is holy then our values and our actions should lead others to Christ. If we become more holy and more like God as we interact with him, then surely in the same way as other people interact with God through us, they too should start to become more holy like him.

I heard a story from one of my young people the other week that seriously struck me. Laura told me that only a few months before a friend of hers had started to come to our church simply because she saw something different in her Christian friend. Two years earlier Laura had been very different. Her friends had told her that they liked her because she wasn't like all those other Christians, she smoked, drank and spent lots of time with guys. Hearing these words coming from her friends' mouths she suddenly realised that this was not a positive thing, this was not what it was meant to be about. She had always thought that she could be in the world so that she could lead people from that world into God's world but instead what had happened was that her friends had thought that she was a part of their world and not the eternal world. Stepping back from this conversation Laura started to make huge changes in her life. Now she is leading her friends to faith simply by being different, by being countercultural, by pulling in God's gravity.

ACTIONS SPEAK LOUDER

Over recent years I have had great amounts of fun being involved in mission weeks around the country. Several of these missions have used the famous words 'Actions Speak

Louder than Words' as their slogan (we Christians like our slogans). It's true our actions do speak louder than words, but somehow many churches are still doing mission on the once-a-year model. How can the actions of a church, once a year, really make a lasting impact on a community?

As we grow up there are uncles or aunts who we only see at Christmas or large family occasions. These are the family members I try to avoid, as I haven't a clue what to say to them, I don't know them and the reality is they don't know me either. The people we spend time with are the people we know and trust. What makes us think that seeing people only once a year will cause them to come to faith?

Our whole lives should be mission and not just the occasional weekend. It should be more like a pinball machine; our faith is real when it is bouncing off the relationships and people we meet on our daily journey around the table. Our lifestyle of holiness should be something that draws others into conversation. With the mission weekend method, we are forcing people into having conversations with us and seeing that we are there with our street dramas. If we are holy people who 'are' mission and living a life of joy, peace and forgiveness what we are doing is allowing people to see Jesus and ask about him when they are ready on their terms and on their turf.

Many of us act as though mission is like standing on the roof of a building throwing off cricket balls at people to see if we can knock as many passers-by out with the gospel of freedom and love as possible.

EMMAUS

Mission should be more like that of the journey found in Luke 24. After Jesus' death and resurrection he joins two men on the road to Emmaus, which was a small daughter village outside Jerusalem, quite often used by visitors coming for the Passover (a daughter village is a small village birthed out of another village). When he meets them, Jesus keeps his true identity secret just long enough to spend some quality time with the men without them asking silly questions like 'How did you do it?'

The road from Jerusalem to Emmaus was around seven miles long. If the average human walks at 2.5 miles per hour and we gauge these guys as fast walkers of 3.5 miles per hour, then this journey would have been around two hours.

Early in the conversation the two men are talking about the events in Jerusalem days before and from their perspective, tell Jesus all about himself. The two men are in essence talking about the real world they live in and are discussing the news of the day. They describe Jesus as a prophet or teacher and are willing to unpack what has happened. Seeing their willingness Jesus starts from the beginning and tells them how everything fits into the Moses, Abraham and Isaiah story. He explained in the words of the day all about how he fulfils Scripture and how this impacts their news. Jesus used the world he was living in, to tell the story of the eternal rescue plan.

Their eyes were then opened and they saw who he was, they realised that it was Jesus who had been unpacking life with them. At this point he disappeared.

Telling the other disciples the two men start to call Jesus Lord. These two men start the story calling Jesus teacher and end the journey calling him Lord.

Teacher.

Lord.

Don't we all do this when we come to faith? We move from calling Jesus a wise teacher to calling him our Lord.

Jesus walked the Emmaus road to help unpack the story of what God had done. He spent time with them and when they trusted him he went Bible 'flip-mode' almost like a new form of martial arts.

Kung-fu Bible, or Bible-fu.

With the holy book's message flying all around them they then start to see that it's a story of a loving, creative Father trying to help people reclaim their humanity and rebuilding the world around them.

We need to be doing the same. We need to live lives that are open so that people can grow to trust us. We need to journey with people not for short times but for long journeys in the real world and in real life. This includes the good times and the bad, whatever state we find them and ourselves in.

THEIR STORY AND THE ETERNAL STORY

As we develop friendships and trust with people, we can help them to unpack the reality of life so that they can see how meeting Jesus can change their lives. We need to help them see that their story fits into the eternal story. Mission isn't about how trendy your church is, or how welcoming your team are, although all of this is important. Mission is about journeying with people and helping them see that they fit into the eternal story of the God who made them and ultimately saves them.

My prayer for us all is that we come to realise that we are already in the story, we are living it and that we need to see that it is our job to help others see themselves in it. I pray that we can start to live lives orientated to the Father's blessing so that we might lead others into it. Let us start to be the holy people God created us to be, and may we set out to unpack for the world the true reality of his holiness and that holiness is a continued commitment to starting again,

and again . . .

. . . and again.

LIVING IT OUT

- When was it you went from calling Jesus teacher to Lord and Saviour? How did this affect the life you were living?

- How often are you watched because of the way you live? Why do you think people don't watch you more often than this?

- Can you see how a life of holiness can be evangelistic? Has there been a time in your own life or in that of a friend where holiness has caused others to ask what's the difference between you and them?
- What is it in your own life that you need to stop doing or start doing that will make more people watch you carefully? What are the easily achievable things that you can start doing today?

- We are called to be salt of the earth. If we understand this to be acting like an antiseptic how do you think this would look in day-to-day living?

- How do you think this would look on a global church scale?

FURTHER READING

The Irresistible Revolution by Shane Claiborne forced me to look at this issue deeply when he calls us to live lives that are antiseptic in a damaged world. This book was the most challenging one I have read to date.

The Powers that Be by Walter Wink also looks at how Christians need to be a part of rebuilding the world. It's not linked to evangelism but you can see how this message is evangelistic.

The Naked Christian (subtitle: *Taking Off Religion to Find True Relationship*) by Craig Borlase talks about how to live this naked life when the rubber hits the road.

EPILOGUE:
RADICAL
HOLINESS |11

NO BLUE EYES AND BLOND HAIR IN SIGHT

Since starting the journey of being a Jesus lover and then of writing this book I have found a Saviour that was much more than just the blue-eyed, blond-haired, sash-wearing hippy. Jesus is not only the Saviour of the world but also a holy revolutionary. Even though we know in our hearts that Jesus came to open the eyes of the religious leaders of the time and to revolutionise how they saw this holy God, few Christians see the true depth of his revolution. It's a revolution that undermined every structure and power this world has ever seen.

If we are to live as people who are orientating ourselves to the Father's blessing and realising that we are his children then this has to have a radical and powerful impact on our worshipping communities, our lives and the world. For many Christians act like Jesus was a nice guy, who preached some nice sermons and spoke lots about loving each other. Even if at a basic level he was like this, how come we can't even love each other?

Jesus said 'love your neighbour' (Mt. 22:36–40), but so many Christians don't even speak to their neighbours and I include myself in that. The words that left Jesus' mouth were provocative yet we teach them as if they were just nice sayings.

Is it that we are not familiar with what Jesus actually said, or are we merely not reading the challenging bits? Jesus was a revolutionary teacher, radical prophet, provocative preacher, controversialist and the relentless opponent of the religious establishment.

JESUS' LOVE WAS POLITICAL

Jesus was holy, he had orientated himself to his Father which meant that he was never nasty or critical. His orientation made him love the unloved and keep loving without end until it lead to his death, death on the cross. And because he loved, through his direction to his Father's heart his message became political.

His teachings in Matthew 5:38–42 about being slapped on the other cheek[23] and walking the extra mile were all about helping people reclaim their humanity from Caesar Augustus' power and a misused law court.[24] Teachings about loving your neighbour were about doing away with the racism against the Samaritans. Jesus taught that there was another world that we could live in, a world where everything was orientated to the heart and passions of the Father. This was never about a world to live in once we have died but a word possible here on earth right now. The Jews had a phrase for this, which was *'Olam Ha-Ba'* which means to live here now as in the age to come. Essentially living here on earth as it is in heaven or living here orientated to the Father's kingdom.

Jesus taught about bringing change to humanity's view of YHVH the good Father. He spoke about changes to the way men and women saw each other and interacted, changes to the world's view of the underdog and the poor, changes of ethics to the old order of things, replacing it with a new order. He came to bring a new covenant, a new agreement, a new promise, a new government, a new baptism, a new community, a new church, a new culture and a new society. And this was called God's kingdom here on earth.

In this kingdom everyone is equal and everyone is loved, not just the religious believers. It is a kingdom where there is no more fear, no more pain but lots more grace, forgiveness, mercy and love. And did I mention love?

Jesus was a man who would not bow down to the authorities of this world and religious conformity.

Jesus preached a revolution.

Jesus preached a non-tolerance of double standards.

Jesus preached a non-tolerance of oppression.

Jesus preached a liberating gospel.

Jesus preached a forgiving gospel.

And when Jesus preached he was more than happy to stir up anger in the religious people, because it was the religious that were more off track than anyone else. I'm so glad we have worked all of that out and that we never get off track. If only.

He was never only a messiah, or a divine payment, he was never only a prophet coming to make the comfortable feel uncomfortable, he was never only a priest representing man before God and representing God before man but also a revolutionary. Jesus came to tear apart the old ways with a view to orientate the whole church back to his ways.

A NEW LOOK AT AN OLD TRUTH

For many Christians, this is a new look at the Jesus they hear being taught about each Sunday but it is all there in the Bible. When it says in John 11:35 that Jesus wept at his friend Lazarus' grave, this wasn't only because his friend had died, but because he knew this was never as God had intended the world to be. In God's design there was no pain, no death and no crying. Jesus knew that this world was becoming a living hell for many of us and that was never in the plan. Jesus came to bring a little of heaven to earth, God's kingdom to earth. *Olam Ha-Ba*.

Jesus' pattern of revolution runs deep. On one occasion, Jesus healed a blind man by mixing dirt with spit and putting it in the man's eyes (Jn. 9:6). Such an act was in direct defiance to the Jewish law that stopped you from working, let alone healing on *Shabbat* (Sabbath). Yet Jesus intentionally shattered this tradition publicly and with absolute determination. Jesus ate food with unwashed hands under the judgmental gaze of the Pharisees, again intentionally defying their out-of-date tradition (Mk. 7:1–20).

LEAVING RELIGION FOR JESUS

If you are going to direct your whole life to the Father and his ways then you will naturally become a true disciple of the revolutionary from Nazareth which means you will need to realise a few things. It might mean that you end up going to places that aren't nice. Jesus hung out with those who had life-threatening illness, had professions religious people wanted nothing to do with, and who would be seen as 'those people'. Following Jesus will lead you to 'those people' whom most of society want to hide away. Being a follower of the revolutionary from Nazareth does not mean eating organic and drinking fair-trade tea, although both of those things are good. Being a follower means going to the people who need the help. For example, giving bags of clothes to the homeless collections is a good start. But orientating your life to this Jesus actually means going to the homeless and giving them what they need direct: the other way is still trying to keep them at arm's length.

Being a follower is about being that antiseptic, being that salt of the earth, being right there next to the pain and hurt, living life with them and welcoming them on the journey with you back to orientation.

Orientating to God's kingdom and his blessing is dangerous, please be warned. You may end up changing your political views, your heart may become bigger and you may start to want to see the world changed. And if you start to do this you will eventually evoke a question all revolutionaries get asked. It is the same question that was asked of Jesus' disciples while he walked this earth. That question is 'Why do your disciples break the tradition of the elders?' (Mt. 15:2). What they are essentially being asked is 'Why don't you do what we do, us religious folk?'

Our response needs to be, because I do what the revolutionary does, I'm leaving religiousness behind for orientation to Jesus.

Let's stop being like the performing monkey and start orientating ourselves to God because we know that this is the only thing that will change the world.

TWENTY LESSONS LEARNT

1. Holiness is not about performance but our orientation.
2. We need to make sure we know which side of the hill the sun comes up.
3. Being in tune with God will help us know what he is doing.
4. We are God's sons and daughters: we are loved: we give him joy.
5. Therefore we need to start acting like it.
6. Satan will try to tell us we don't know who we are but we need to trust that our Dad's the king.
7. We are free and no longer slaves.
8. Love wins every single time.
9. Our Father is perfect, whole and holy and will never change.
10. The performance is over, we need to be free from the dancing.
11. We need to put on Christ's clothes.
12. Bible, prayer and worship are fundamental to holiness.
13. We need to dump our filth and move on, it's a past event.
14. The cross is a present reality.
15. We need to forgive because we have been forgiven.
16. We have the power to set people free from what they have done to us.
17. Humility is confidence correctly placed in God.
18. Our ego will try and get in the way.
19. We need to live totally free naked lives, no holding back because others will see.
20. Holiness is not about living a cheap version of life but a more real, more full eternal life now.

APPENDIX:
JESUS AND JUDAISM |

Jesus never claimed to be a Christian. In Greek the word is *christianos*, which means a 'follower of Christ'. Early followers of Jesus were simply known as followers of 'The Way' (The church's oldest title seems to have been The Way. References to this can be found in Acts 9:2;19:9) and it was not until later that the term Christian was used. I often have to stress that Jesus and his followers were Jews who felt strongly that they should follow the Torah, the first five books of the Bible. Those of us who aren't Jewish would have been known to those early followers of Jesus as Gentiles, people who were outside the family. The Bible says that the Gentiles have been grafted onto the special relationship between God and the Jews (see Rom. 11:17,19,23,24 for more detail). Jesus was a devout Jew but also was concerned about the hypocrites who were distorting the faith. He was intent on helping people see that they had deserted the traditions that were Judaism's foundations.

So if Jesus was Jewish why aren't we Jewish now? The early Christians did all they could to try and hold this faith together. They worshipped in the Jewish temple and they still taught the Torah and lived out *Shabbat* (Sabbath). The early name for Jesus' followers, The Way, was a term used by the Jewish rabbis to refer to the Torah. These early believers understood that they were teaching a more authentic belief in the Torah and that Jesus was the fulfilment of all the prophetic words about the *Mashiach* or 'Messiah' within it.

The problem came during the second Jewish war against the Romans. Around 135 AD when the war was at its worst, the issue of the *Mashiach* became divisive. The leader of the Jewish revolt, Simon Bar Kokhba, was hailed as the *Mashiach* by one of the leading rabbis of the day, Rabbi Akib. This decision left the early followers of Jesus in the position of having to accept Simon Bar

Kokhba as the *Mashiach* or part ways and stay true to their belief that Jesus was the *Mashiach*. It was at this point they separated from the Jewish faith and accepted the need for a separate faith, which became Christianity.

The Torah is the first five books of the Bible and is the most important part of Judaism. The Torah is best translated as 'teaching' or 'instruction' but is quite often translated as 'Law'. It can be known by other names such as 'The Five Books of Moses' or even 'The Law of Moses'. The names of the books within the Torah are pronunciations of the original Hebrew. Genesis in Hebrew is *Bereshit* which means 'in the beginning'. Exodus in Hebrew is *Shemot* which means 'names'. Leviticus in Hebrew is *Vayyiqra* which means 'and he called'. Numbers is *Bammidbar* meaning 'in the desert' and Deuteronomy is *Devarim* meaning 'discourses' or 'words'. The Hebrew names are taken directly from the first words found within the opening verses of each of the books.

READING LIST

Borlase, Craig, *The Naked Christian* (London: Hodder & Stoughton, 2001).

Bridges, Jerry, *The Pursuit of Holiness* (Milton Keynes: Authentic Media, 2004).

Bridges, Jerry, *The Discipline of Grace* (Colorado Springs: NavPress, 2006).

Brown, Dan, *The Da Vinci Code* (London: Corgi, 2004).

Chambers Mini Dictionary (Edinburgh: W & R Chambers, 1990).

Claiborne, Shane, *The Irresistible Revolution* (Grand Rapids: Zondervan, 2006).

Common Worship (London: Church House Publishing, 2005).

Fee, Gordon D. & Stuart, Douglas, *How to Read the Bible for All Its Worth* (Grand Rapids: Zondervan, 2003).

Hicks, Peter, *Encounters with God* (Milton Keynes: Authentic Media, 2006).

Jenson, Philip, *Graded Holiness* (Sheffield: Continuum, 1992).

Kushner, Lawrence, *Jewish Spirituality* (Woodstock: Jewish Lights Publishing, 2002).

Lamm, Norman, *The Shema: Spirituality and Law in Judaism* (Philadelphia: Jewish Publication Society of America, 1998).

Mahaney, C.J., *Humility* (Colorado Springs: Multnomah, 2005).

Mahaney, C.J., *Living the Cross Centered Life* (Colorado Springs: Multnomah, 2006).

Manning, Brennan, *Abba's Child* (Colorado Springs: NavPress, 1994).

McLellan, Vern, *Wise Words and Quotes* (Carol Stream: Tyndale House Publishers, 2000).

Mitson, Eileen (ed.), *Songs of Freedom* (Oxford: Lion Hudson, 2005).

Page, Nick, *The Bible Book* (London: HarperCollins, 2002).

Rufus, Rob, *Living in the Grace of God* (Milton Keynes: Authentic Media, 2007).

Sproul, R.C., *The Holiness of God* (Carol Stream: Tyndale House Publishers, 2000).

Wallis, Jim, *God's Politics* (Oxford: Lion Hudson, 2006).

Wink, Walter, *The Powers That Be* (New York: Bantam Doubleday Dell, 2000).

Yancey, Philip, *What's So Amazing about Grace?* (Grand Rapids: Zondervan, 1997).

Yoder, John Howard, *The Politics of Jesus* (Grand Rapids: Eerdmans Publishing Company, 1996).

ENDNOTES |

¹ The early Jewish Christians understood this world to be created by the hand of a holy God and that everything within it pointed to that holy Creator. Because everything was created by YHVH they believed that we could never say 'I have a secular job, not a religious job' as, at the end of the day, nothing could be secular because everything was sacred through God. Their spirituality held to the idea that wherever they looked they were able to see the power of God around them and therefore needed to allow themselves to tune into God so that they could sense his presence. Jewish rabbis believed that everything was sacred and that God's fingerprints are all over the world that we are in. Many Jewish teachers pushed this further and believed that at certain times and in certain places it was almost like God goes into 'flip mode' and reveals something to us.

² www.figleafforum.com

³ This is a reference not to my present state as I have a full head of hair, but to my birth state.

⁴ A straight man that embraces grooming, refined tastes in clothing, excessive use of designer hygiene products and is in touch with his feminine side.

⁵ Rabbi Lawrence Kushner in *Jewish Spirituality* says that key to understanding the Torah is that the events of the Torah are true, not because they happened but because they happen every single day. This book is fantastic for the development of understanding how the events of the Bible are actually the events we all experience and enter into every single day.

⁶ For more on this topic try reading a book called *Graded Holiness* by Philip Jenson. It's a little heavy as it is based upon a PhD thesis but if you're interested it's a great read.

⁷ New Living Translation.

⁸ If anyone knows what the book is called or where I can get a copy, I would be thrilled to hear from you. I lost my copy some years ago in a house move and I really miss it.

[9] 1 Samuel 13:19.

[10] The name *rabbi* is someone who is a Jewish teacher or more literally the 'great one'. The word rabbi originally comes from the Hebrew root word *'rav'*, which in biblical Hebrew means 'great' or 'distinguished'. By tradition a man obtains his title rabbi only after he has completed the tough learning program in the codes of the Torah or Law. The rabbi would be expected to know the Torah and the other books of the Old Testament off by heart.

[11] This is a major understatement, I had to go hide in their loo just to catch my breath and then eat very little the next day.

[12] Nehemiah 8:10–12.

[13] The opening response from the Eucharistic prayer, also known as communion, from *Common Worship*.

[14] William Temple was actually the ninety-eighth Archbishop of Canterbury. He was born in 1821 and ordained a priest in 1847, he was then made headmaster of Rugby, then Bishop of Exeter in 1869. Some time later he became the Bishop of London and eventually Archbishop of Canterbury, dying in 1902. And was quite famous for having chickens. This quote comes from *Wise Words and Quotes* by Vern McLellan (see Reading List).

[15] Theology is literally the 'Theo' – God 'logy' – study. Theology is the study of the nature of God and religious belief, and religious questions. This quote is from *The Essential Holmes* (Chicago: University of Chicago Press, 1997).

[16] Cris Rogers' translations of Matthew 26:74.

[17] This view of holiness and righteousness was also held by a Jewish school of thought called Gnosticism that thought the study of God and his origin would bring you spiritual enlightenment and gain you redemption, releasing the divine 'within us'. This Gnostic thought is walking severely on dodgy ground and certainly not on biblically correct ground. I wouldn't want anyone to think what I am saying is linked in any way with this.

[18] It is thought that he had either ten or eleven wives. We are unsure of the exact number due to lack of decent historical records about the later wives. His first few wives were Doris, Mariamne I, Mariamne II, Malthace, Cleopatra, Pallas, Phaidra and Elpis, after this details are a little foggy, but it is thought that he possibly married one of his cousins and a niece.

[19] From his large amounts of wives Herod is thought to have somewhere in the region of forty-three children.

[20] During underwater archaeological digs in the late 1970s, archaeologists stumbled across highly sophisticated use of concrete blocks near the breakwater offshore of *Caesarea*. It is well known that the Romans had developed such techniques, but before this find, it was never thought that concrete was used on such a massive scale as this project. The main ingredient in the concrete was volcanic ash, which is now thought to probably have been imported from Mount Vesuvius in Italy.

[21] These seven heavenly virtues are: chastity, self-control, charity, diligence, forgiveness, kindness and humility.

[22] 1 Thessalonians 4:12.

[23] When Jesus talks about offering your other cheek he is making a comment about your humanity. Traditionally you would not do anything with your left hand as this hand was used for unclean acts, so you would have to slap the person with your right hand. It was also traditional that you would slap the person with the back side of your hand. This was a normal way of showing the person was inferior to you. Romans would back slap Jews, masters would slap slaves and men would slap women. It was about showing authority. So when Jesus says offer your other cheek, he is telling the person to now hit you with their right hand on your right cheek. Which if you try it is impossible to do as a back-handed slap. To hit the right cheek with the right hand now had to be a fistfight. This

suddenly isn't a fight with an oppressor but is now a fight with an equal. You are no longer the underdog. Essentially the person is saying try hitting me again because your first slap didn't humiliate me and if you're going to do that let's do it as equals. Jesus is claiming that the humiliated can reclaim their humanity at the same time as stripping the other of his. For more on this you must read *Jesus and Non-violence* by Walter Wink (Minneapolis: Fortress Press, 2003). It's an amazing book with some great ideas on non-violent means of dealing with evil in the world.

[24] Walter Wink spends whole books looking at this subject. He argues that there are three general responses to evil oppression. 1) Do nothing about it. 2) Deal with violent retaliation. 3) The way of non-violence. Walter Wink talks about Jesus' politics being that of a third way. A way that uses humour and non-violence to undermine evil oppression and to shed light on the evil that it is. Read more about this in *The Powers That Be* (see Reading List).

ND - #0093 - 270225 - C0 - 198/129/12 - PB - 9781850787822 - Gloss Lamination